BEYOND THE BARS
The Zoo Dilemma

'As a child I accepted happily the idea of zoos as a natural part of life. As an adult I have been forced to think again. This book explains why.' – *Michael Aspel.*

'A vital contribution to the cause of wildlife protection everywhere which will hopefully convince anybody in doubt as to the urgency of the situation.' – *Bryan Forbes.*

'There is no excuse for keeping wild creatures in captivity for our amusement. I hope this book hastens the day when all animals live their lives as nature intended.' – *Tony Soper.*

Pole Pole 'in the wild'. (Artist's Impression)

BEYOND THE BARS

—

THE ZOO DILEMMA

Edited by

Virginia McKenna * Will Travers * Jonathan Wray

THORSONS

THORSONS PUBLISHING GROUP
Wellingborough, Northamptonshire

———————

Rochester, Vermont

First published 1987

© THORSONS PUBLISHING
GROUP LTD 1987

British Library Cataloguing in
Publication Data

Beyond the bars: the zoo dilemma.
  1. Zoology, Economic
  2. Animals,
  Treatment of
  I. McKenna, Virginia
  II. Travers, Will
  III. Wray, Jonathan
  179′.3   HV4708

ISBN 0-7225-1363-1

Printed and bound in Great Britain

10 9 8 7 6 5 4 3

Contents

Acknowledgements 7

Foreword by Prince Sadruddin Aga Khan 9

Introduction by Sir Christopher Lever 11

Past, Present – Future Indicative 25
Virginia McKenna

Science Grows and Beauty Dwindles 41
Bill Jordan

Keeping Species on Ice 55
Mary Midgley

Whales – a poem by Spike Milligan 66

Some Thoughts on Animals in Religious Imagery 67
Richard Adams

Lobbying for Parliament 85
Roland Boyes MP

Can the Earth Survive Man? 97
Mark Glover

The Last Leopard in the Cape – a poem by Spike Milligan 113

Individuals in the Landscape 115
Baron Hugo van Lawick

Wild Life Conservation – a Modern Concept 129
Arjan Singh

Amen – a poem by Spike Milligan 144

Conservation as a Human Problem 145
Kieran Mulvaney

Inadmissible Evidence 161
Bill Travers

Index 205

Acknowledgements

Dear Reader,

Book acknowledgements are often the page that most people skip. A few florid sentences or a dry list of names cannot really do justice to the contributors. So, in this case, I thought I would try to write a personal letter to you explaining just how unusual *Beyond the Bars* really is.

No contributor to this book works for Zoo Check – they all have highly specialized full-time jobs that take up almost every waking moment. But, somehow, they 'made' time. Each chapter represents many days – sometimes weeks – of careful thought, writing and re-writing. And for what reward? To communicate to you their own philosophies, and their concerns for wildlife and nature.

I believe very much in visual impact and so it was very important that the writing in this book was supported in a significant and compelling way. This, I believe, has been achieved thanks to the many wonderful photographs given to us by a number of other animal organizations and individual photographers. It is impossible to list each one, but I would especially like to thank Hugo van Lawick for his marvellous cover photograph as well as for the others which illustrate his chapter, to Ian Dobbie for his evocative photos of Pole Pole and to Wolf Suschitzky for his unforgettable 'Guy the Gorilla'.

Not only photographers but artists as well. Original work by Robert Gillmor, Mandy Shepherd and Tessa Lovatt-Smith. Artists for whom the world of animals, in all its dimensions, inspires their creativity.

These are the people you 'see' in this book. There are others you will not. Each an important and indispensible member of the team – Tricia Holford, Nina Wiltshire, Carrie Baird, Janet Booker, Marjorie Russell, Jan Adams, Liza Fury.

Above all my gratitude to Thorsons and in particular John Hardaker for inviting us to undertake this project and for the subsequent encouragement and support.

Animal organizations are often criticized for spending too much time arguing amongst themselves, and too little time campaigning for the things they hold so dear. But perhaps as significant as anything written in *Beyond the Bars* is the unity of compassion, care and concern for the world we live in that every contributor has expressed.

Yours sincerely

Virginia McKenna

Virginia McKenna

Zoo Check
Cherry Tree Cottage
Coldharbour
Dorking
Surrey RH5 6HA
(Reg. Charity No. 296024)

Bellerive Foundation

PO Box 6 · 1211 Geneva 3 · Switzerland · Telephone: (022) 46 88 66 · Telex: 42 98 35 MURO CH

THE PRESIDENT

22nd January, 1986

Rarely before, if ever, has the subject of zoos been treated
with such depth and insight. Zoo Check, under the tireless
leadership of Virginia McKenna and Bill Travers, as well as
Thorson's Publishing Group, deserve congratulations for the
way they have succeeded in bringing to the public, in such
compelling and readable form, an impressive array of
well-documented arguments covering all aspects of the
debate.

Above all, the book succeeds in avoiding the tendency to view
zoos in isolation rather than as just one link in a chain of
interrelated issues having global repercussions. The chapters
that follow contain a wealth of information to convince even
the most sceptical of readers that traditional justifications
for zoos - ranging from conservation to educational value -
may now be seriously challenged as obsolete - not only on
ethical but also on purely scientific grounds.

The time has surely come to explore new methods involving,
for example, increased emphasis on the establishment of
national parks for the study and protection of indigenous and
endangered species in their natural habitats as well as the
promotion of comprehensive conservation education through
increased resort to modern audio-visual techniques. These
methods have a clear advantage over most zoos when it comes
to bringing home the ultimate futility of preserving wildlife
without parallel efforts to preserve the fragile ecosystems
on which all living creatures depend. For the animals it is a
question of survival. More and more, as this book highlights
so forcefully, we are coming to realise that on their
survival depends our own.

We can perhaps do no better than to reflect on the example of
one particularly enlightened zoo which has installed a mirror
behind bars. Visitors can look into this and read the caption
"Homo sapiens ... species endangered by its own doing"!

Sadruddin Aga Khan

Sadruddin Aga Khan

Illustrations by Tessa Lovatt-Smith

Sir Christopher Lever

Introduction

Sir Christopher Lever worked in the City as an accountant and a stockbroker before becoming a director of his family textile business. Two of his books, *The Naturalized Animals of the British Isles* (Hutchinson, 1977) and *Naturalized Mammals of the World* (Longman, 1985), have become the standard works on the subject. A companion to the latter, *Naturalized Birds of the World*, is due to be published by Longman in 1988. As well as being a Consultant for Zoo Check, he is Vice-President of the International Trust for Nature Conservation, and has recently been appointed Chairman of the British Trust for Ornithology's National Centre Appeal. He is also a trustee of several other conservation and animal welfare organizations. For many years he has been a regular visitor to north and east Africa. He lives in Berkshire, where he runs a flock of Soay sheep and feral goats.

The 'zoo dilemma' in the title of this book has arisen as a consequence of recent trends in contemporary life; it is a manifestation of current thinking.

During the past quarter of a century or so there has been a great upsurge in people's awareness of the marvels of the natural world. This has come about largely as a result of the very high standard of wildlife films on television, which have brought the sight and sound of wild animals in their natural surroundings into people's homes, and have opened the public's eyes to the wonders of animal intelligence and behaviour. The increasing popularity of 'package' wildlife safaris has put the viewing of exotic animals in their own countries within the budget of an increasingly large number of people. Together, this has led to a burgeoning realization of the consequences, both actual and potential, of man's rape of the world and its resources, and to a growing determination to do something about it before it is too late. Conservation has, in stockbrokers' idiom, become a 'growth industry'. This has all contributed to a change in the general attitude of man in his relationship with other animals.

In her opening chapter, Virginia McKenna describes the catalyst (the death in 1983 in London Zoo of the elephant, Pole Pole) that transformed her from the ordinary animal-lover that she had for so long been to the activist whose 'breaking point' had been reached, and which led in the following year to the formation of Zoo Check.

Although it would be wrong, as she points out, to sentence all zoos to a blanket condemnation, or to say that no species are suitable for keeping in captivity, it is equally foolish for the directors of zoos to claim, as they so often do, that all such establishments are today totally different from those of the 'bad old days', and that they are now universally models of enlightened management. Some undoubtedly are (the Jersey Wildlife Preservation Trust and San Diego Zoo in California spring to mind), but the vast majority are still – despite their vehement denials to the contrary – simply places of public entertainment.

In a previous book I have written: 'the reintroduction to the wild of endangered species bred in captivity is increasingly becoming accepted as the only justification for keeping wild animals in confinement. The umbrella pretexts of "education" and "scientific research" are no longer – if, indeed, they ever were – valid.' Better still, of course, than breeding endangered species in captivity, is the construction in their native habitat of fenced sanctuaries, where they can live and breed in security until it becomes possible to return them to the wild. Virginia McKenna describes the construction in Kenya of the Tsavo Rhino Sanctuary, which was partially funded by Zoo Check. Other sanctuaries for black rhinos in Kenya (in Nakuru, Nairobi, the Aberdares and Meru) are currently being built by the Rhino Rescue Trust. In *New Scientist* (26 September 1985) I advocated the formation of similar sanctuaries for the Sumatran rhino in Indonesia and Malaysia.

Are we, as Virginia McKenna suggests, ignoring our indigenous wildlife in favour of captive exotic species? The Royal Society for the Protection of Birds, the Nature Conservancy Council, the Royal Society for Nature Conservation and the National Trust, among other organizations, do what they can to encourage people to watch our native animals in their natural surroundings, but more still needs to be done to educate the public to the glories of our native wildlife.

The British have for long enjoyed a world-wide reputation as a nation of animal-lovers. We react, as Virginia McKenna rightly says, with horror to *active* acts of cruelty against both wild and domestic animals, yet remain apparently unmoved by the *passive* cruelty of imprisonment in zoos. Most of us would probably agree on the cruelty of perpetually confining a *domestic* dog to a kennel, but many remain unconcerned by the sight of a permanently caged *wild* animal. This ambivalent attitude is hard to understand.

'There is no doubt in my mind,' Virginia McKenna writes, 'that a huge and unstoppable tide of public opinion demanding change is already taking place.' That this is undoubtedly true is confirmed by the ever increasing number of newspaper reports and magazine articles condemning the keeping of wild animals in captivity. On a personal note, since my involvement with Zoo Check, more and more of my acquaintances have confessed their secret dislike of and reluctance to visit circuses and zoos – secret because such a view has, until fairly recently, been regarded as unfashionable and even somewhat eccentric.

For Bill Jordan, the catalyst that led to his 'breaking point' was his first visit to Africa in 1964. For the previous fourteen years he had found fulfilment in his work as a vet at Chester Zoo, but on his return he saw his patients for what they really were – mere parodies of the magnificent creatures he had observed in the wild. I have myself noticed the same reaction among people whom I have taken on safari.

'What then' asks Jordan, 'is the purpose of a zoo? What are the reasons for keeping animals captive?' To these questions zoo directors reply that they are places of education, entertainment and conservation, and that they carry out important biological research. But the educational facilities and contribution to conservation provided by the majority of zoos is negligible, and the value of biological research conducted on animals kept in unnatural conditions is, to say the least, questionable. Only the claim of zoos as centres for public entertainment stands up to examination.

Zoos also assert, as Mr C. G. C. Rawlins, then Acting Secretary of the National Federation of Zoological Gardens, did in *BBC Wildlife* magazine (May 1984), that 'television and films, however beautifully and realistically they portray the wild, are still no substitute for seeing a live animal.' Having for some years been a regular visitor to Africa, where I have been privileged to see wild animals in their natural surroundings, I am left in no doubt whatever that the splendid natural history films now being produced give an incomparably truer picture of the wild animals they portray than does the caricature of the same creature seen live in a zoo.

'This,' Jordan continues, 'poses two further questions; are zoos essential to conservation, and are there acceptable standards for captive animals?' On the first point Jordan feels we should keep an open mind. On the second, he draws attention to the deficiencies of the Zoo Licensing Act 1981 which, although it sets minimum criteria for zoo management, does not and cannot eliminate or address itself to all the problems. For example, it imposes no control or minimum qualifications on zoo staff, on whom the welfare of the inmates ultimately depends.

Housing, diet and health (both mental and physical) are the most important aspects of animal management in zoos. With the question of mental health and zoo animals' behaviour we come, as Jordan says, to 'the core of the problem which is the subject of vigorous debate.' Zoo directors claim firstly, that because their animals appear (physically) healthy, breed well, and are (sometimes) long lived, they must, *ipso facto*, be 'happy'; and secondly, that anyway surely a life behind bars, free from danger and the necessity of constantly searching for food and shelter, is preferable to the hazards of freedom? Anyone who has observed the psychotic, stereotyped, aberrant behaviour of many zoo animals can be in no doubt as to the fallacy of the former point. The latter is an argument I find particularly irritating and naïve; what would the answer to the same question be from a 'lifer' in one of our gaols? To the cynic who accuses me of facile anthropomorphism I reply: 'what proof have you that an imprisoned wild animal has feelings different from those of a human being?' Freedom is a most precious commodity – and, I submit, not only to man. Thomas Jefferson asserted that among the inalienable rights with which man is endowed by his Creator is that of Liberty: why should the rights of wild animals be regarded as inferior?

'In the wild,' as Jordan says, 'an animal's time is predominantly taken up with avoiding enemies, seeking food and procreation.' These are its natural functions. 'These occupational necessities disappear in captivity.' By what right does man deprive it of them?

What are conservationists aiming to conserve? Are whole ecosystems, isolated habitats, genera, species or individuals to take precedence? What is special about a species? What priority does a species have if its interests are found to conflict with those of individuals or the biosphere? Can a wild species saved from extinction in a zoo, with the intention of eventually returning it to the wild, be kept indefinitely in a kind of limbo? If so, would it remain a species in the normally accepted sense of the word, and have the same values that species characteristically have? Or does that value depend on it fulfilling its role in a larger system? If it is unlikely that such a species can ever be successfully returned to the wild, does the remote possibility justify the stresses imposed on its present captive members? If the gene-pool of a captive species proves too small, is it to be augmented by the removal from the wild of further individuals, with the accompanying wastage and upheaval that this invariably incurs? Or must those genes that *are* available somehow be made to cope? Is 'bizarre' too strong an epithet to describe human, or other, surrogate motherhood? These, and other equally stimulating questions, are asked and answered by Mary Midgley in her pertinent and thought-provoking chapter.

The problems that can arise when attempts are made to re-establish captive-bred species in the wild (and even the cruelty that this can sometimes entail) are also discussed. As Mary Midgley points out, the practice of breeding animals in captivity for reintroduction to the wild has many exacting demands that are not normally a part of standard zoo management. It is right that such difficulties should not be minimized. It is not without significance that the majority of the various successful reintroductions of endangered species to the wild have been made not with animals bred in zoos, but with those bred by other organizations involved in captive-breeding programmes. Even if zoos were able to breed animals in captivity for subsequent release in the wild, we are faced with another dilemma. Does the breeding of endangered species justify the keeping of non-endangered ones to provide funds (by fee-paying visitors) for the necessary research?

At some time or another, and by some group or society, animals have, since recorded history, been the subject of worship by man, and animals and animal imagery have been an integral part of every one of the world's great religions – including Christianity.

Human beings have always identified deeply, in both thought and imagination, with the other creatures with whom they share this planet. Mankind has never been without a deep consciousness of other animals as an important component of the divine order, and as a consequence has always had feelings for them that can best be described as wonder and reverence. What conclusions regarding man's relationship with other animals today follow from this truth must remain a matter for individual decision, but to Richard Adams and, I suggest, to many others also, they are, *inter alia*, that the luxury fur trade (involving both wild-caught and farmed animals), circuses and zoos are inherently evil. All of them cause animals both physical and mental suffering for no justifiable reason and, which is even worse, also rob them of their *dignity* [Adams's italics] and natural animality. 'That dignity,' Adams concludes, 'is inseparable from our own . . . if we rob the animals of their dignity we are, by that act, lowering ourselves too.'

The catalyst that led to Roland Boyes's 'breaking point' was the humiliating sight of an elephant in chains in the Belle Vue Zoo in Manchester, and the even greater shock of witnessing for the first time the degrading (both to observers and participants) spectacle of performing animals at a circus.

For many people, circuses, and the attitude of their owners, are even more contemptible than are zoos and the conduct of their proprietors. I have before me, as I write, a cutting from *The Times* newspaper of 24 November 1986, in which Mr Richard Chipperfield of the circus family is quoted as saying, following criticism of the alleged confinement of three elephants for three months in a 40 foot by 8 foot metal transport container, that 'those three elephants are worth £100,000. We look after *stuff* [my italics] like that.' Comment on such an attitude, if accurately reported, would be superfluous.

Boyes describes how, when elected a Member of the European

Parliament, events there stimulated in him an interest in animal welfare, and how, as a British Member of Parliament, he became convinced, as a result of strong anti-vivisection lobbying, of the evils of animal experimentation.

These issues, however, did not obscure Boyes's preoccupation with the fundamental cruelty of imprisoning animals in zoos, and he describes how the Zoo Licensing Act has contributed in some measure towards improving conditions in these institutions. 'The long-term goal of abolition of zoos,' however, Boyes continues, 'must never be relegated to a low priority. The *right* [my italics] to imprison animals has to be constantly attacked.'

There may, of course, Boyes concedes, be a case for the creation of specialized establishments where genuine scientific research is undertaken, and where saving endangered species from extinction is a priority. But, and this cannot be too strongly emphasized, such places are not zoos, nor are zoos substitutes for them.

Far better, where that is possible, is the designation of more National Parks as sanctuaries, where rare species can live and breed unmolested. Unfortunately, however, present policy tends towards mass despoilation of the ecosystem rather than to its conservation. The International Union for Conservation of Nature and Natural Resources (IUCN), among other organizations, has spoken out against such a course of action, and has pointed to the vital necessity, if mankind is to survive, of a change in attitude. The following is the IUCN definition of 'conservation' (*World Conservation Strategy*, 1980): 'the management of human use of the biosphere (that is, all living things) so that it may yield the greatest sustainable benefit to present generations while maintaining the potential to meet the needs and aspirations of future generations.' Development, especially in the so-called third world, is inevitable, but there is no reason why it should not occur in association with conservation. Let us pray that man's instinct for self-preservation may yet save him from himself.

Boyes concludes by giving some useful ground-rules for potential parliamentary lobbyists, and by discussing the scope for extra-parliamentary non-violent action. The use of violence by the 'rent-a-mob' lunatic fringe he rightly condemns as being invariably counter-productive. Do those misguided people, I wonder, who release rats and mice from laboratories and mink from fur-farms, ever stop to consider the harm they are doing by, in the former case, subjecting their fellow human beings to an increased health hazard, and in the latter by putting at risk our native wildlife through the liberation of a voracious alien carnivore.

During the infinitesimal period of time during which *Homo sapiens* has occupied and held dominion over the earth, he has wreaked havoc on the natural resources and life-forms that have evolved over millions of years.

'Man's list of "crimes" against nature and the natural world,' writes Mark Glover, 'is enormous and frightening.' It includes the extermination of innumerable species of animals and plants; the deforestation of millions of acres of rainforest; the depletion of valuable and finite mineral deposits;

pollution of the atmosphere; and the formation of 'acid-rain' through the burning of oil and other fossil fuels, which has resulted in an increase in carbon dioxide, with a marked impact on the 'greenhouse effect' which controls the earth's temperature. 'There can be no doubt,' Glover continues, 'that we are transforming the paradise that our species emerged from into a wasteland.' This appalling situation has arisen largely through the shortsighted attitude of commercial interests, which think only of themselves and care nothing for the needs of future generations.

Although animal welfare organizations, in one form or another, have been with us for a century and a half, concern for the environment has only come to the fore in the last few decades. The newer and more radical animal and environmental pressure groups have frequently failed, due, Glover contends, to a combination of lack of experience in political lobbying, a distrust of parliamentary procedures, frustration over their opponents' apparent delaying tactics, shortage of funds, and lack of public support. 'Some organizations,' Glover continues, 'are prepared to break national laws set by governments, maintaining that higher moral or natural laws exist.' This may or may not be so, but who, I ask, are such people to claim that it is *they* who are right? By deliberately and flagrantly flouting the law of the land (all too often by violence) they inevitably alienate a large proportion of the public on whose goodwill they ultimately depend; far better, albeit slower, to campaign vigorously for a *change* in the law rather than to break it. The latter leads only to anarchy.

The use of *non*-violent direct action, as practised by such organizations as Greenpeace, is not only more effective in achieving the results desired but also in obtaining the important support of 'the man in the street', at whom elected governments are constantly looking over their shoulder, and on whom the benefits of change will ultimately devolve.

The power of individuals collectively is immense; if enough people shun zoos, circuses, safari parks, furs and animal-tested cosmetics, more will be achieved than by a whole host of pressure groups. The same principle of the power of the individual applies to the desecration of the environment. We hold our own destiny and that of future generations in our hands.

'If one accepts,' writes Hugo van Lawick, 'that other creatures have the same or very similar emotional feelings as humans, then it becomes easier to imagine the suffering they are subjected to when kept in captivity and used in experiments.'

Man's attitude to other animals was originally formed during the early period of evolution, when prehistoric man and some other species preyed on each other and/or competed for food. Man finally emerged as 'top dog' when he acquired the ability to use implements as weapons (chimpanzees, man's closest relations, are the only other animals known to do this), and the feeling of physical and mental superiority that this engendered fostered in man a belief that the 'lower' animals existed solely for his benefit and pleasure.

If the money spent on zoos formed for man's entertainment was instead channelled into conservation of animals in the wild and their habitats, many of the rare species now in captivity would no longer be endangered. 'There is little doubt,' van Lawick rightly contends, 'that the falling attendance at zoos is due to the effect of wildlife films, and the greater awareness that this has created of the artificiality of zoos and the immorality of keeping wild animals in captivity.'

If only for his own selfish sake, man *must* learn to conserve the world's natural resources; the day may come, says van Lawick, when a pandemic will ravage mankind that could have been cured by some extinct plant. Has that day, I wonder, already arrived, with the devastating scourge of Aids? Even if some remedy or preventative for this dreadful disease is eventually found, who can say that it might not have been discovered sooner, with the consequent saving of many lives, had man not previously exterminated from the earth so many plant species?

'A good knowledge of animal behaviour,' writes van Lawick, 'is likely to stop anyone wanting to kill animals. . . many hunters in Africa as they become older (and wiser) stop hunting, and are often embarrassed about their hunting days.' This, from my own personal experience, is undeniably true. (Sir Peter Scott discusses this dilemma in a chapter entitled 'The Ultimate Sanction' in his autobiography *The Eye of the Wind* (Hodder and Stoughton, 1961)).

In conclusion, van Lawick reiterates the argument that if enough individuals do not visit zoos, do not wear or buy wild animal skins or products, and do not keep wild animals as pets, it will become impossible to ignore the groundswell of public opinion. It is often argued that wild animal products can be an important source of foreign exchange for poor third world countries; this argument would be negated if richer countries made more funds available for wildlife conservation in poorer ones, where the creation of further National Parks with the help of this cash injection would result in a compensatory growth in foreign revenue from the resulting increase in tourism.

Although most conservationists, I think, accept that the term 'wildlife' includes all living things (both animals and plants, which are, indeed, inseparable, through their inter-dependence on each other and through the vital role that habitat conservation plays in the preservation of animal forms), Arjan Singh suggests that there is a clear distinction between the 'inanimate' environment (flora) and 'wildlife' (fauna), and claims that although there is a valid argument for preserving, for example, trees, on the grounds that they are essential to the well-being of man, the preservation of 'wildlife' because it may be of some future use to him is a 'miserable and meaningless cliché'. Perhaps he has not read the IUCN definition of 'conservation' that I have quoted above.

As with other contributors, Arjan Singh points out that man has, down the ages, looked on animals as existing solely for his benefit, whether as objects of the chase or as a means of amusement in circuses and zoos, where both entertained and entertainer lose their vital dignity. Although he concedes the existence of some 'good' zoos (he cites in particular that at San Diego in California), the claims of most others as centres of conservation, scientific study or education, are (as by other contributors) rightly condemned as spurious.

'Animals must be saved,' Arjan Singh continues, 'for their own sake and not because the public will, hopefully, decree that it should be so.' Although in an ideal world this may well be true, I feel that, as Roland Boyes suggests, changes in our attitude to the treatment of animals and the environment will only be brought about through a corresponding change of opinion by the public, and by popular demand.

The dismissal of hunting as having no place in wildlife conservation (a view which many conservationists undoubtedly share) should, I think, be accompanied by some account of the claims of its proponents: these are that the funds arising from licence and other fees lead to an increase in local employment, including that of anti-poaching game-wardens; that the payment of a levy on every animal killed encourages local communities to regard wildlife as a valuable natural asset, and thus deters them from reclaiming wildlife habitats for agricultural purposes; that the meat provides a useful source of protein to local people; and that official hunting parties act as unpaid game-wardens against poaching gangs. Whether or not these claims are considered to have any validity they are, I think, worth at least discussing.

Arjan Singh concludes with a moving and fascinating first hand account of his personal successes in reintroducing captive-bred tigers and leopards to the wild in his native India.

Kieran Mulvaney examines in depth the consequences, both actual and potential, that arise from the rape of one of the world's most fragile ecosystems – tropical rain forests. These include the loss of new medicines and agricultural crops; soil erosion; deregulation of the earth's temperature through an increase in carbon dioxide caused by the burning of felled timber, which could eventually result in the melting of the earth's ice-caps, followed by a rise in the sea-level and disastrous world-wide flooding; and a change in climate that might drastically affect rainfall patterns, with serious consequences for world agriculture.

It is impossible to say how many individual species of animals and plants have been lost as a result of deforestation, but it has been estimated that some ten per cent of the world's known plants, and the same percentage of birds and mammals, are currently in danger of extinction; thus evidence to support the claim by zoos that they are valuable breeding centres for endangered species for reintroduction to the wild is seen to be sorely lacking; the number of species that have been successfully re-established is infinitesimal when compared with the vast number known to be in danger of extinction.

Illustration by Tessa Lovatt-Smith.

Zoos also sometimes argue that, as a result of habitat loss, they are the only repositories of so-called 'museum species' – those animals saved from extinction by captive-breeding, but for which there is no hope of return to the wild, since no suitable habitat for them remains. This argument, too, Mulvaney rightly condemns, since it places the wrong priority (that of individual species over habitats and ecosystems) on conservation, and incorrectly implies that the worst effect of mass habitat destruction is the loss of a few wild animals and plants, whereas in fact it is the wholesale starvation and even death of millions of human beings.

Thus, conservation is not simply a case of saving species from becoming extinct, and the contribution to it claimed by zoos is seen to be negligible. 'I remain firm in my conviction,' Mulvaney concludes, 'that saving the *wild* [my italics] is the only practical means of conservation.'

In his concluding chapter, Bill Travers movingly narrates, in dramatized form interspersed with apposite quotations, the unhappy life and untimely death, after many years of incarceration, of one of the best-known of latter-day innocent 'prisoners of circumstance'.

'One of the most striking phenomena of our time,' wrote Nigel Barley in the catalogue of the 1986 exhibition 'The Animal in Photography', 'is the way in which Western Man is engaged in tentatively renegotiating his moral relationship with animals.'

This attitude is exemplified by the following quotations from this book, with which I conclude my Introduction. One is by Bill Jordan: 'I feel uneasy in the presence of a captive animal, even when I cannot say it is suffering. Even in the zoos thought to be the best, captivity cripples the animal.' The others are by Virginia McKenna: 'It is the sadness of zoos which haunts me.' 'We should not be alarmed by the change of attitude and feeling that is sweeping through the world. We should only thank whatever god we believe in that it has, at last, begun.'

Mandarin Ducks by Robert Gillmor.

The Mandarin Duck

Revered for aeons in your Orient home,
Symbol of love and true fidelity.
To we poor Europeans you were once,
Prosaically, the humble 'Chinese Teal'.
Now we accord you your true worth
And name you for a Chinese potentate.
A riot of colours, rainbow-touched, you show,
As if an artist's palette had been spilt
Upon your glossy plumage.
In England, now your firm adopted home,
We welcome you, fair stranger from afar;
Long may you grace and gladden our green land.

Christopher Lever 1986

The Mandarin Duck is a native of China, the Far Eastern USSR, Korea and Japan. In Oriental literature it has for long been revered as a symbol of marital bliss and fidelity.

Those birds now established in the wild in England, where there may be as many as 1,000 pairs, are all descended from stock bred in captivity in the present century by private aviculturists, by whom they were subsequently released; they probably exceed in number the entire population in eastern Asia outside Japan.

Working with lions. (Bill Travers)

Virginia McKenna

Past, Present – Future indicative

In March 1984 Virginia McKenna, well-known award winning actress of stage and screen, and her husband, Bill Travers, founded Zoo Check, a non-profit making Trust dedicated to preventing all types of abuse to captive animals and promoting international support for the conservation of wildlife in its natural environment. She is perhaps best known for her portrayal of Joy Adamson in the 1964 film *Born Free*, and it was this that sparked off her active interest in wildlife. She has written two books: *On Playing with Lions* (Collins, 1966) and *Some of My Friends Have Tails* (Collins, 1970).

I do not think it would be unreasonable to say that everyone has a breaking point; a limit beyond which pain, intimidation, loneliness and unhappiness become intolerable. When that limit is passed people either go under or they take positive action, fight back in whatever way they can. This may appear a rather extreme way to explain what happened to me in 1983 – particularly as the breaking point was reached not by something that happened to me, but something that happened to an elephant.

In 1983 I had been a professional actress for 34 years and had had, on several occasions (*Born Free, Ring of Bright Water, An Elephant Called Slowly*) the good fortune to work in films with and about animals. All through my life I have had a deep love of and concern for animals and supported, when I could, causes which strove to eliminate cruelty towards them. After 1964, when my husband Bill Travers and I made *Born Free*, my interest in animals developed rapidly. Nobody could have worked for almost a year in Kenya, in the company of George and Joy Adamson, and not have been influenced by their philosophy or been inspired by their own relationship with other species.

I had always disliked the idea of captivity in zoos and circuses – animals behind bars and performing in the ring. The idea that man seems able to do what he likes with all the other creatures on this planet disturbed me. But my breaking point had not arrived.

It happened quite suddenly in October 1983, with the death of Pole Pole the young elephant at London Zoo – the elephant Bill and I had worked with in a film in Kenya in 1968. That unnecessary death, the media response and the subsequent public outrage was my catalyst. No longer could Bill and I be individuals – voicing our concern and apprehension about man's treatment of animals. We could not because we realized, at that moment, that we were not alone. From the letters we received we became aware that hundreds and hundreds of people felt the same. They, too, had been waiting for their catalyst – and here it was.

It is not often that a person, after they reach the age of fifty, gets a second chance at life. That an all-absorbing, fascinating interest opens up new and unexplored dimensions. A new purpose recharges one's batteries. But this is what has happened to me. It is not conducive – let me add – to a relaxed and easy existence! When you challenge the 'experts' – and you yourself are not a scientist – you lay yourself open to scathing criticism – and you have to learn, fast. You have to collect around you a team of people who are scientists and who can advise you. My years as an actress had prepared me well for criticism and, in any case, my determination to become a more positive force in the struggle against animal exploitation was unquenchable. Those same critics poured scorn on Zoo Check – the organization six of us started in 1984 – saying it was the brain-child of a bunch of emotional cranks and that it would be a nine day wonder. Over three years later Zoo Check is still here – stronger than it has ever been, supported by people all over the world and a force to be reckoned with. My only regret is that my breaking point did not arrive twenty years ago.

There are two photographs in front of me. One is of a drawing of an elephant by Matthew Paris, presented to King Henry III in the thirteenth century by St Louis. Its front left leg is tethered to a stake by a short chain. The other is of an elephant in Milan Zoo, taken by my husband, Bill Travers, in the twentieth century, September 1986. Its front left leg is tethered by a short chain.

As foolish as it would be to say that all zoos in the world are cruel and terrible places (a few zoos are able to look after certain species reasonably well), it is equally foolish for some directors of zoos to affirm (which they constantly do) that zoos these days are completely different – that animals do not suffer, are not deprived, are no longer in cages. They cannot have been to the zoos in Milan, Rome, Battersea, Basildon, Flamingoland, Sestri Levante, London, Salon, Canton, Kathmandu, Haifa, Athens . . .

However zoo directors try to describe the conditions in which their animals live by calling them displays, or exhibits, in 'enclosures', one thing is

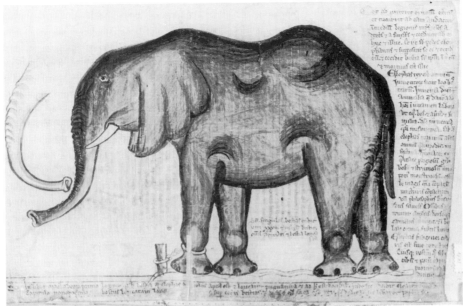

Above *Thirteenth century.*
(Courtauld Institute of Art)

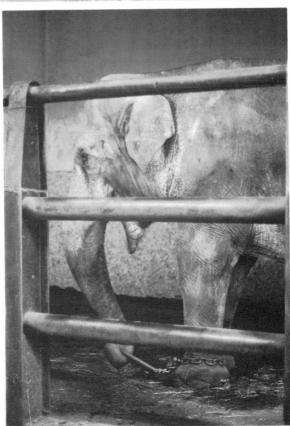

Right *Twentieth century.*
(Bill Travers)

certain, the animals are not free. But they are *safe*, it is argued. Safe from attack, safe from death by starvation, safe from being hunted, safe from possible extinction. In a simplistic sense all this is true. After all, the human prisoner in jail is also safe – from attack or starvation. But zoo animals are innocent prisoners and over the past three or four years I have seen too many of them in different countries, surviving in appalling conditions, to accept these specious arguments.

There are, as I have said, exceptions, and some zoos look after some species in such a way that the animals do not appear to feel stress. Unfortunately, these zoos are in the minority.

In Britain alone there are approximately 260 zoos (including bird gardens). To maintain standards of care for the animals we now have the monitoring structure of the Zoo Licensing Act – and yet conditions and situations are passed and accepted, which in the view of thousands of people, including scientists, should not be tolerated.

For example – from a scientific survey carried out on behalf of Zoo Check in 1985 by marine biologist Paul Horsman ('Captive Polar Bears in the UK and Ireland') it was discovered that 12 out of the 20 polar bears in these zoos

A kind of survival. (Bill Travers)

were psychotic, some severely so, and that 60 to 70 per cent of cubs died before the age of one year (in the wild it is 10 to 30 per cent).

Yet in spite of these and other disturbing facts a government enquiry, sought by Zoo Check, was deemed unnecessary. Must we assume from this that psychotic behaviour is acceptable? Perhaps a government report on polar bears following so swiftly the government report on Dolphinaria would be seen as high-level lack of confidence in zoo management – this might be confusing in view of the government's grant of £8.5 million (spread over three years) to London Zoo where planned improvements include the replacement of the Mappin Terraces with a 'North American Tundra' exhibit. This will be inhabited by various arctic species – including of course, polar bears.

However, now the lid of the box has been prised open it must never be allowed to close. If an investigation into one species can reveal these problems, for the sake of the hundreds of other animals who may also have become mentally unbalanced because of their captive conditions, it is vital that more scientific investigations take place.

Supportive as most people are of the conservation movement, we should

Chart from Captive Polar Bears in the U.K. and Ireland. (P. Horsman)

Psychotic polar bears – Bristol Zoo 1986. (Rita Wren)

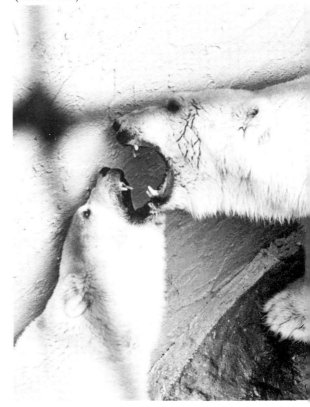

THE BEAR FACTS

ZOO	Number of bears	Years in captivity	Degree of stereotypy
BRISTOL	Nina (F) Janina (F) Misha (M)	27 11	★★★ ★★ Severe
CHESSINGTON	Bonnie (F) Clyde (M)	? 4	0 ★
CHESTER	Sabrina (F) Amos (M)	19 20	★★ not seen
DUDLEY	Pipiluk (M) Mosha (F)	20 21	★★★ ★★★
EDINBURGH	Barney (M) Mercedes (F)	9 2	★★ 0
BELFAST	Dudley (M) Wash (F) Tumble (F)	? 5 5	0 Both females in maternity dens
DUBLIN	One male, One female Unnamed	5+ 5+	★★★ ★

★★★=*obvious stereotypic behaviour (the technical term for pointless, repetitive behaviour).*
★★=*moderate stereotypic behaviour.*
★=*possible stereotypic behaviour.*

Left and below *Rail sucking.* (Bill Travers)

not accept unequivocally the zoo's stated role of 'Ark' in this issue. The great umbrella of conservation, education and research under which zoos shelter is a myth. Those zoos with genuine rehabilitation programmes for a few species, such as Jersey and San Diego, provide a convenient image for other zoos, most of which do not even keep endangered species. The elephant on the chain; the mad polar bear; the pacing tiger; the giraffe continuously sucking the top restraining bar of its enclosure, the monkey with the tip of its tail stripped to the flesh from over-grooming, the crazy fox leaping in a circle round its two and a half by two metre cage – these are not part of the conservation programmes. These are zoo animals for whom there can never be a 'return to the wild'. The truth is, most zoo animals can never be returned to the wild. These are the zoo animals which the zoos encourage us to bring our children to see so that they may learn about them. These are zoo animals who, through captivity, have become and remain damaged. The years of research that zoos have done have not been able to prevent it.

The boredom of the zoo animal reflects on the visitors. They have paid to be entertained so they start calling out, waving, trying to provoke a passive animal to get up and do something – to walk about, eat, react to them in some way. Only when the environment stimulates the animal to behave in some natural or unnatural way will the public then want to stay and watch. (The large gorilla enclosure at Jersey Zoo is a case in point.)

We are told in zoo publicity, that we should come to the zoo 'for a good day out', that the zoo 'firstly is a place for fun and enjoyment'. Some people

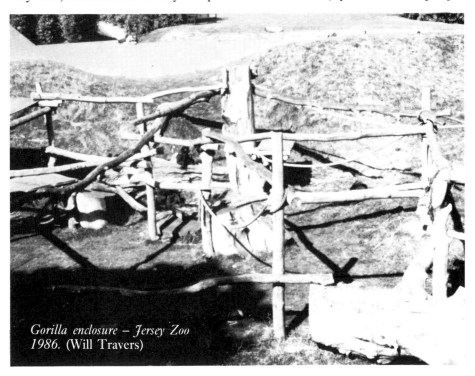

Gorilla enclosure – Jersey Zoo 1986. (Will Travers)

never question this, they take it on trust; after all, zoos have been around as long as any of us can remember. So we take our children and our children accept it because, after all, we, as adults should know. But do we, and why do we want to see animals in zoos? Perhaps it is our need to have 'contact' with other species; a need to reassure ourselves that we, the human race, are in control. Perhaps it is just a hang-over from the days when we gazed in awe at the fearsome and strange creatures brought back from foreign lands by intrepid explorers. It is possibly a mixture of all of these. In those days, we knew nothing else; we could make no comparisons. But times are changing and most zoos cannot adapt fast enough to keep up with the new awareness stimulated by brilliant documentary films like *Kingdom of the Ice Bear, Life on Earth, The Wild Dogs of Africa, The Year of the Wildebeest, African Elephant, The Flight of the Condor,* the BBC's *Nature* programmes and the Anglia TV's *Survival* series.

We are beginning to learn about the natural history of our planet and all the forms of life it supports through the eyes of some truly remarkable wildlife photographers. Through their films we know how animals live, behave and die. We learn about their social and territorial requirements, which makes the label on a cage – 'Leopard, Reema. We bite fingers' – seem trivial, bizarre, a terrible mockery.

The idea of animal 'adoption' in zoos beguiles people into believing they are really doing something for conservation. You can buy a giraffe's front foot, a tapir's ear, a lion's whisker – you can take your pick. In reality you are helping to pay the zoo food bills. However, you can only fool some of the people some of the time. As more schemes for genuine conservation in the wild become a reality, people are starting to realize that these are the projects they should all be supporting. Black rhinos doomed to live in London Zoo forever will serve no significant purpose for the preservation of the wild rhino in its natural environment; living museum species and desolate African plains empty of wildlife will be sorry legacies for our grandchildren.

It is the sadness of zoos which haunts me. The purposeless existence of the animals. For the four hours we spend in a zoo, the animals spend four years, or fourteen, perhaps even longer – if not in the same zoo then in others – day and night; summer and winter. Have you ever thought about zoos in winter? Some zoos do not open at all. No visitors. Unrelieved monotony. Hard, cold weather. Certain exotic species cannot be left outside. The prison walls close in. In one of the new zoo concepts, which combines animals with the funfair, it is even worse. Animals are just part of the sideshow. This is not conservation – and surely it is not education. No, this is 'entertainment'. Not comedy, however, but tragedy.

In the zoo the world is topsy-turvy. Man decides which animal will live and which will not, which will be sold, which will mate with which and which animals will be hand-reared. Sometimes young are hand-reared because the mother rejects them – she herself, zoo-bred and possibly hand-reared has not learned what to do from her own mother. At other times young are

It is the sadness of zoos which haunts me.
(Bill Travers)

removed in order that they can be handled for the summer season. We have all seen the lovely 'cuddly' lion and tiger cubs. What then? After the season where do they go? Other zoos? Circuses? Misfits in an already artificial world.

Zoo curators manipulate, 'manage', cross-breed (do we *need* 'ligers'?) in their efforts to attract more visitors. But as a more discerning public reduces the takings on the 'gate', the funfair, the 'cuddly' animals, the dimensions of the zoo which have nothing whatsoever to do with education, conservation and research, but only with entertainment, mushroom before our eyes – while the wild areas of the world that we desperately need to preserve (the huge grant to London Zoo would ensure proper management of a Game Park for many years), fall victim to our greed, our indifference or our failure to anticipate the future.

I cannot imagine anyone living in the nineteenth century, or even the early part of the twentieth century, believing they had a 'right' to see a lion, or an elephant. We have no 'right' to see anything. We have no 'right' to expect other creatures to be imprisoned for life for our entertainment – even for our 'education'. Not to look at them and certainly not just to smell them – (yes, even that has been put forward as an argument). Why should we, who have vastly increased opportunities to learn about the world – through travel and through film – have more 'rights' than those people who, years ago, never had those advantages? After all would we expect another Taj Mahal to be built in Piccadilly Circus?

It would be quite wrong to assume from what I have just said that I wish to deny people the thrill and excitement of seeing live animals. That is an experience I wish everyone could have – as long as the animals are not deprived and are not suffering. However, I suggest we should start off from a totally different premise. If we do not want to live in a world inhabited almost entirely by humans, how can we ensure that other creatures survive. How can we share the world with them in such a way that they can enjoy some of the freedoms that our own species values so highly. Freedom of choice, of food, of partner; freedom to follow the behavioural patterns for which each species has evolved; freedom of communication. Even the freedom 'to work' for survival.

To ensure these 'freedoms' we have to protect habitat – the ecosystem – so that animals can remain in their own environment. Where this has become increasingly difficult because of poaching or man's destruction of that habitat, then selected, completely protected and supervised areas must be allocated within the countries concerned. The first working example of this new idea, for the black rhino, (apart from animals preserved on privately owned ranches) is the Tsavo Rhino Sanctuary in Kenya. In this experiment an initial four square kilometres (one square kilometre for each rhino) have been enclosed with solar-powered electric fencing. Four rhinos are *in situ* and, at the time of writing, the area is being extended to sixteen square kilometres. A special ranger force patrols the area and, although it is not total freedom it is, in my opinion, a more humane and intelligent approach

Destined for the Tsavo Rhino Sanctuary. Senior Warden, Bill Woodley, discusses with the author a rhino with a future. (Bill Travers)

Rhinos in the wild. (Hugo van Lawick)

A greeting in the wild. A dog fox and fallow buck touching noses in the New Forest, England.
(Eric Ashby)

to the problem of conservation of endangered species. Sanctuaries of this kind can be established on a world-wide basis – allowing animals to remain in the environment and climate for which they are suited, and educational programmes and facilities for scientific study can be integrated into each conservation area.

I think we have been brainwashed into believing that our own native wildlife is less interesting, less exciting than exotic animals from other countries. We have been encouraged to expect too much. Should we try to look at the issue from the animals' point of view we would soon realize that indigenous sanctuaries and nature reserves allow us to watch and study our wildlife in a far more fascinating way and give us a genuine opportunity to have contact with nature.

The RSPB (Royal Society for the Protection of Birds), the World Wildlife Fund, Earthlife and the Zoo Check Charitable Trust have got it right in this respect, in that they work to preserve habitat, and by doing so they preserve the creatures within it. With the pressure from human demands increasing every day no one is saying it is an easy task, but there is no realistic alternative if we want neither a 'concrete' planet nor to deprive ourselves of the spiritual refreshment contact with nature and animals can bring.

As a nation we have, in general, an enormous empathy with animals. We react with horror to stories of cruelty – slaughter of seal pups, massive killing of whales, trapping for fur, dog fights. All these are dramatic issues where blood is spilt and lives are lost.

In the zoo there appears to be no such drama, and so little emerges to

The spiked walls of an elephant enclosure. (Bill Travers)

provoke our reaction. Apart from the odd story of a 'cull' because numbers are too great, the collapse of a giraffe, the death of a young elephant ('heart attack' usually being given as the cause) the public learns little of behind the scenes events. But what about captivity itself? Where we have evidence that this causes stress and suffering – is this not cruel? The argument that the majority of animals are captive-bred and know nothing else is not relevant. How thin is our own veneer of civilization and sophistication; how near the surface our territorial, familial and more primitive instincts. We are deeply concerned with the well-being of our dogs and cats – domesticated animals. We would consider it cruel to confine a dog permanently in a kennel. Yet we visit zoos where hundreds of wild animals are kept permanently in the equivalent of a kennel. It is as if we, like the animals, become trapped within the zoo concept and we cannot see beyond the bars. We forget that wildlife in zoos is still wildlife.

It would be unrealistic to expect zoos suddenly to disappear from our society, but there are far too many of them and far too many keep the kind of animals that suffer from living in inappropriate captive conditions. However, there is no doubt in my mind that a huge and unstoppable tide of public opinion demanding change is already taking place. After all, the zoo issue is not in isolation. Vivisection, fur farming, intensive food production, hunting, habitat destruction, sea and river pollution, acid rain – separate but inter-related issues posing moral questions which passionately concern huge numbers of people. They realize how human interference is not only destroying our environment but is losing us the chance of co-existence with other species.

We should not be alarmed by this change of attitude and feeling that is sweeping through the world. We should only thank whatever god we believe in that it has, at last, begun. It is not controversial, it is logical and humane and everyone who wants to can be part of it. Of course, it is not always easy – reacting against one's parents and teachers does not lead to a peaceful life either! But in the past had we not challenged and questioned, nothing would have changed – we would still have slavery and children down the mines. People, however, do become alarmed by 'animal rights' issues. Stories of violence and intimidation erase all too quickly from our minds the efforts of those people and organizations which work in a less dramatic way for a better life for animals. As far as voicing one's criticisms of zoos is concerned it is quite straightforward. We have complete freedom of choice. Where we find conditions in a zoo unacceptable we can choose not to visit it. We can write strong letters of protest to the zoo, the local council and the Department of the Environment. We can make our voices heard with little hardship to ourselves and with increasing benefit to the animals in captivity which have no freedom of choice. No freedom. No choice.

As the number of voices grows, change will inevitably come about and the worst zoos will be forced to close – the animals, where possible, absorbed into other 'collections' until they die. I say 'where possible' because no one should be under the illusion that zoo animals just remain there until they die

The look in their eyes. (Bill Travers)

peacefully of old age. As Mr Colin Rawlins (former Director of London Zoo) is quoted as saying: 'Animals have to be put down from time to time because of incurable disease or injury; senility, *a surplus of breeding stock* (my italics) – and the fact that we are absolutely unable to place them in another suitable collection.' The reality of life in the zoo is that death often comes before its time – to the healthy, the young and the newly born.

Sometimes the anger I feel towards those establishments, and the people who condone the perpetuation of the kind of captivity I am fighting against, chokes me. Sometimes when things get rough I feel frustrated and hopeless; the proverbial brick wall seems thicker than ever, and my voice, a very small one, shouting against the wind. But then, in my mind, I see the animals in the zoos. The bear in an indoor cage four metres by three; the solitary monkey chained within its concrete pen; birds so confined that flight is impossible; the jungle cat crouching in the doorway of its wooden box inside its tiny concrete cage. I see the look in their eyes. It is a look I cannot forget, which I will not betray and which will follow me for the rest of my days.

Bill Jordan

Science Grows and Beauty Dwindles

Bill Jordan MVSc, BSc, MRCVS, MIBiol, is a founder member of the British Veterinary Zoological Society and its secretary for several years, he is Director of the People's Trust for Endangered Species, one of the founder members and a director of Zoo Check, a trustee of Care for the Wild and The Donkey Sanctuary, a Council Member of the RSPCA, secretary of the Veterinary Specialist Group of the Species Survival Commission and has recently been a delegate of the International Whaling Commission for Britain. He had his own practice for 16 years, was consultant clinician to the government of Iran for six years, and for 16 years was veterinary consultant to Chester Zoo. He still consults on wildlife problems pertaining to conservation throughout the world. His books include *Care of the Wild* (Macdonald, 1982), *A-Z Guide to Pet Health* (Constable, 1986) and *The Last Great Wild Beast Show* (Constable, 1978) – a discussion on the failure of British animal collections.

He was of medium build, slightly overweight, with a good complexion from spending time outdoors. He looked hot in a dull tweed suit as he sat on the edge of his swivel chair.

The oak desk had curios from various parts of the world. There were two horned skulls on the walls of the room and several photographs of wildlife taken in Africa. On top of a filing cabinet in one corner a potted plant drooped. He spoke quietly with a hint of urgency in his voice. 'My zoo is well kept and clean. The animals are fed on a balanced diet wherever possible.

As you know, animals do not like variety in their diet. We call a vet whenever an animal is sick or injured.'

He was looking at me intently for some reassurance that I, a vet, should understand him. 'I have a dedicated bunch of keepers who love their animals. We have a good breeding record. Many animals live much longer in my zoo than in the wild. We employ an education officer because one of our main aims is education of the young. It is the best way to help conservation.'

The window behind his chair was open and the breeze was rustling the leaves of the tree outside. A pigeon flew into the branches and cooed.

'Zoos provide a service for conservation. They are necessary for the education of the public,' he intoned.

The breeze carried the scent of early summer, and he did not know. He had not heard the pigeon – his mind was closed by the facts and arguments he had absorbed long ago. Moments of joy in nature and natural things rarely, if ever, touched his soul. He could discuss stress, suffering and adaptation to captivity. He would never know what freedom is, for he himself was captive.

I had been like that. For 16 years I worked in a zoo and my spirit had emptied as my mind filled with facts, experience and other people's theories. 'Science grows and beauty dwindles', said Tennyson.

Though I did not know it at the time, I was struggling with an unconscious internal conflict between my conviction that science can provide all the answers, and my spiritual need for the mysterious. Reason told me that science would eventually explain everything and this seemed to make me emotionally sad.

When I began working in Chester Zoo in 1950 I was on contract to keep the animals healthy. I was given freedom to visit the zoo as often or as little as was needed, and to take charge of diets and management. Chester Zoo was growing fast and the Founder Director, Mr Mottershead, was an innovator who stood head and shoulders above other zoo directors at that time. It was an exciting era. Tranquillizers had not been discovered nor had most of the antibiotics used today. Little was known about the dietary requirements and diseases of many captive species. Many animals died soon after capture, and birth and survival rates were low. Zoos were consumers of wildlife.

Almost every day brought a new problem. We were learning all the time. It was impossible not to grow attached to some individual animals. A leopard befriended me and would rub its head against my legs asking to be scratched behind the ears. An elephant quickly learnt that a display of affection towards me would be rewarded by tasty morsels of biscuits or dates. For a time, a young female chimp would embrace me in adoration – or so I thought. I have since begun to wonder if they were simply responding to my feelings towards them, or even taking advantage of my sympathetic attitude.

Chester Zoo was the first to break away from the cage type of exhibit. Most species were kept in groups, or at least pairs, and were given more space than in the traditional zoo. The chimp exhibit was unique at that time;

Polar bear compound – Chester Zoo 1985. (P. Horsman)

the indoor accommodation opened out onto small areas of land which were bounded by a water-filled moat, instead of a wire cage. Family groups of chimps would sit on these islands, watching visitors. The Polar bears had been given a pool in a compound, which was larger than those of most other zoos, and larger species of mammals were accommodated in paddocks, for the zoo eventually covered several hundred acres.

More and more young were born to many species and successfully reared. Keepers developed a sense of pride and derived great satisfaction from their work. I enjoyed the challenges, the successes, and even the failures because we were learning all the time and the improvements were visible.

Occasionally a major supplier of wildlife would visit us to discuss future needs and I would question him closely about his life in Africa or elsewhere. His tales of safaris into the bush filled my mind and I vowed that one day I would go and experience it for myself. It was 1964 before that happened.

I flew first to Nairobi and then on to Tanganyika (now Tanzania), to make my base with a friend who lived in Moshi. During the next few weeks I visited the Serengeti, Ngorongoro Crater, Lake Manyara and Mount Kilimanjaro. Africa is like no other continent. One can use words like mysterious, primitive, savage and still not convey the impression, the feelings, the excitement of what it is like to be there.

The morning comes quickly near the Equator and at the first hint of dawn the lion's powerful roar stirs all living things with uneasiness. He roars again and again and yet again, and the birds shake their feathers, stretch their legs and yawn. Daylight is coming quickly now, and suddenly one hears the repeated screech of the fish eagle as he wings his way out over the lake. The gazelle and antelope are on their feet immediately, alert ears pricked and nostrils flared. The giraffe swings his neck round so that the momentum will help him get to his feet – an awkward, difficult manoeuvre. However, once up he is one of the most graceful of animals. The zebra stallion calls out.

Now it is the turn of the elephant to stir. He is afraid of no other animal, except man. The lion's roar means nothing more to him than a call to eat, for the elephant has a gargantuan appetite and wakes up hungry.

Morning is the time for feeding and, being a vegetarian, and having a liking for all sorts of titbits, he must start early. Indeed, this is the time of activity for most animals, for African mornings are cool and inviting. The elephant family gets down to the serious business of filling their stomachs, each one consuming up to 300 kilogrammes of vegetation per day.

I remember one day we were following some fresh elephant tracks. We knew we were close because the dung pats were still steaming. I looked round and could see nothing. Then suddenly what I took to be a shadow on the other side of a small bush moved. I had almost collided with an elephant without knowing it was there. Had I listened more carefully I would probably have heard the faint noise of its tail swinging to and fro against its hide. Ignoring me, it moved on again quietly.

The African midday brings a special kind of stillness. The afternoon heat lies like a heavy blanket on the brown earth. There is no breeze. The huge baobab tree seems to sag. The thorn trees contract, and what green vegetation there is, wilts. At this time most of the animals are resting. A buffalo dung pat moves, stirred by the prodigious strength of the dung beetle as it shifts and breaks down the material. Only the hum of the tsetse fly can be heard and it seems to heighten the silence.

Africa is like no other continent. (Hugo van Lawick)

Those incredible weeks of beauty, grandeur and closeness to nature were an inspiration that will never fade from my memory.

When I returned and looked again at the inmates of the zoo I saw only caricatures. The charm, the challenge, even the sense of achievement had gone. The wildlife was incomplete without its natural environment. In any case, what was it all for? What we see in zoos are isolated bits which our minds try vainly to assemble into something meaningful. Life is not just knowing. It is also feeling, and happiness resides to a large extent in feeling – a feeling of satisfaction or wellbeing or contentment – not simply knowing.

What then is the purpose of the zoo? What are the reasons for keeping animals captive?

Part of the answer lies in the origin of zoos. They developed from menageries which were assembled by showmen to make money by displaying strange creatures to the ever curious public. Even the more traditional establishment zoos, set up to study the many and various creatures of the world, were nonetheless a more sophisticated form of curiosity.

Today many zoos claim much more. They say there is no substitute for seeing the living animal, no matter how good nature films become. Species can only be preserved from extinction if the public at large are motivated. The zoos say that in exhibiting live specimens they do exactly that. Some of the larger zoos now do considerable research into diseases, diet and reproduction of wildlife. Though some is applicable to animals in the wild, much of it is, of course, orientated to captive animals.

Many zoos claim that they contribute to conservation, and point out that some specimens of a few species have been saved by captive breeding, and even returned to the wild. 'Give us the money', they say, 'and we can build zoos that can provide every captive species with space and facilities suitable to their needs.'

This not only raises the question, are they – zoos – an essential part of conservation, but also, are there acceptable standards for captive animals?

The first question cannot be satisfactorily answered by a few examples. We should keep an open mind. However, as far as conservation is concerned, most zoos concentrate on saving a few spectacular species and tend to ignore the habitat and all the smaller less glamorous creatures it contains. For example, zoos can conserve the jaguar while its habitat, the rain forest of South America, is being cut, burnt and cleared for commercial exploitation. At present nothing is being done to conserve the tens of thousands of species that are perishing in the process. If ever the jaguar can eventually be released to the wild, both it as a species and the environment from which it came may be very different.

The problem is that because science reduces and over simplifies – dissects and divides into parts to examine – it destroys the whole that is greater than the parts. It can describe most of the processes that can take place in a living body but cannot explain what life itself is. It can describe

Wildlife . . . (Simon Bicknell)

. . . is incomplete without its natural environment. (Bill Travers)

what happens when a giant tree crashes to the ground in a rain forest, or when a pesticide disperses across the globe, but the effects are too complicated and inter-related for present-day scientists to fully comprehend.

The preservation of a handful of species in zoos, for whatever reason, may simply satisfy emotional needs – not a true conservation imperative.

The second question – are there acceptable standards for captive animals – can be answered in two ways. Both are matters of opinion. The first is factual and scientific, the second philosophic and emotional. Both are valid.

The Zoo Licensing Act, 1981, which came into force in 1984, sets minimum standards for zoo management but does not eliminate or address all the problems. The health and welfare of zoo animals depends on the quality of the keepers, the housing, the feeding and veterinary attention. Most keepers receive no formal training, and indeed, in many zoos, they are simply labourers who keep the cages and pens clean and supply the animals with food and water. As a general rule, keepers are poorly paid and they continue to work in zoos only because they find the work so fascinating. In most zoos there is little requirement for special keeper training and there is no organized structure for advancement in this career as skills and responsibility increase.

Indeed, many zoo owners and managers have insufficient knowledge themselves. There is a rapid turnover of staff. Dedicated young people with an interest in natural history and a devotion to animals tolerate this exploitation for only two or three years, and leave disillusioned, to be replaced by more young enthusiasts. Yet one of the basic necessities of any zoo is the quality of its staff, as the welfare of the individual animal lies entirely in the hands of the keeper.

Housing is another important aspect of animal welfare that leaves a lot to be desired in most zoos. Poorly constructed pens, aviaries and cages, made from inferior quality materials soon begin to decay, and not only present hazards to the animals, in the form of jagged nails, wire, etc., but allow inmates to escape, with the concomitant stress of chase, recapture or destruction. In many zoos there is often no source of power to the houses and cages, so that when the animals are sick and require warmth it is difficult, or even impossible, to provide heat.

In many safari parks, railway wagons are used as housing for lions and other species, usually allowing too small an area for the animals in the enclosure. A typical example in one large zoo was the housing for numerous baboons. Because there were insufficient perches, baboons remained on the ground all night, which must have caused considerable stress as it is quite unnatural for them to do this in the wild. They normally perch in trees or on cliff ledges.

The knowledge of nutrition for zoo animals has improved tremendously in recent years. For some species artificial diets have been formulated that contain all the nutrients, vitamins and trace minerals required. This has substantially improved their health and resistance to disease. However, it is

Baboons normally perch in trees or on cliff ledges. (S. R. Whyte)

just not possible to provide zoo animals with their natural diet and this poses a real problem. The tendency is to feed as cheaply as possible in order to keep the animal in reasonable condition. In other words, there is great reliance on the animals' ability to adapt to this modified diet, and those that do not, suffer and often perish.

It is now legally incumbent upon the zoo to provide veterinary care. Because the animals are often living in conditions of stress, they are subject to stress-related disease. Sometimes they are more crowded than in the wild and so parasitism and disease are more likely to spread from one to another. Injuries are not infrequent. Keepers are rarely trained to recognize when an animal is ill, so regular skilled veterinary inspection and treatment is essential. Yet only a few zoos provide it.

Quite apart from these basic practical considerations we must ask if the mental state of the zoo animal is being considered. How big should the cage or enclosures be? Can the animal fulfil its biological instincts? Is the social grouping correct? Can climbing animals climb, burrowing animals burrow, flying animals fly, and swimming animals swim? And if they cannot – what happens? Is freedom preferable to the security of captivity?

We are now at the core of the problem which is the subject of vigorous debate. The zoo fraternity says: 'Look at our healthy animals. See how much longer they live in captivity. They are breeding well, and are therefore contented.' Let us look more closely by studying the behaviour of captive animals.

The study of behaviour not only involves investigating how behaviour works but also how it develops during the life of the individual, and how it has evolved through the generations. No two species behave alike and there are even variations between individuals of the same species. Much behaviour of animals is determined by heredity though the detail of how it works is not known. We do not know exactly why an animal does something. Does a bird build a nest because it wants to lay eggs? Mankind often unconsciously accepts that animals think ahead as we do. But there is no proof that that is so. Animals may do things that have survival value which to us appear to be a well thought-out plan – for example the squirrel storing food. In reality it may simply be instinct and the animal may not know why it is storing food.

There is also the added problem of not knowing how an animal feels subjectively when it is sad, angry, happy, etc. Behaviour includes all the activities of an animal's effector organs (muscles and glands). The isolated study of these symptoms is included in physiology. The study of the activity of the whole animal is called ethology. Most behaviour is, partly, a response to stimuli. Repeated stimulations can cause a change in behaviour called learning. Learning is usually adaptive i.e. it has survival value for the individual or the species. Accordingly, animals learn to behave in particular ways to ensure the maximum benefit for themselves and the species. For example, some species are territorial and scent-mark their territory to warn off intruders. Many species require a stable social order, often based on dominance hierarchy (pecking order), which prevents aggression arising above wasteful and destructive limits, yet ensures that their young have the opportunity to become acquainted with the facts of social life, with rights, concessions, appeasements and methods of communication appropriate to each. Dominance is determined by ritualistic struggle where major injuries do not occur – a sort of jousting.

Displacement activities are explained by Professor Tinbergen (Nobel Prize winner for his work on animal behaviour), by the concept of central nervous energy – an energy surplus that cannot be discharged through its normal channel will then flow into another channel. An animal attacked by a higher ranking animal will take it out on a lower ranking one. If drives are prevented from expression by conflicting situations – there is no lower ranking animal to attack – the dammed-up excitations spark over, so to speak, to another channel, and the animal may start scratching or grooming or some other activity.

Captive behaviour presents a different picture. Professor Tinbergen says that animals kept in captivity or semi-active captivity, in other words an abnormal environment, often show behaviour that, under the circumstances, makes no sense – it misfires. He says that living is like a tightrope act. There are infinitely more ways in which one can fail than the one narrow road that leads to success. He believes that there are many disturbing signs of malfunctioning in man's behaviour, particularly our social behaviour, which man has learnt to cope with in three ways; firstly by invading more and more land, secondly by living in higher densities, and thirdly by adjusting to a wide variety of new conditions.

Captive animals, on the other hand, are forced to accept abnormal behaviour patterns to which they ultimately may not be able to adapt. For example, aggression in animal species in the wild rarely leads to harm or even to killing, partly because each species has a delicately balanced attack and escape behaviour. However, in the zoo, it is well known that aggression can be exaggerated and often leads to severe injury and death.

The important thing to remember is that the animal's reaction to captivity depends upon its species. Some adapt well whereas others never do. The supreme specialists, animals that have taken an evolutionary risk, are the expert killers like the big cats and snakes, and the diet specialists like the koala and the ant-eater. In the wild between hunting for food they live an easy and relaxed existence so long as their niche remains. They are much more content in captivity than the opportunists, the neophilic animals (literally 'loving the new'), who never relax and are always exploring, always on the move. Even in the presence of an adequate food supply the effects of a restricted environment are extreme, for, however familiar the wild environment seems it is always changing.

Nevertheless, they have social and environmental requirements which zoos cannot supply, and many need the exercise and excitement of hunting. In a zoo the environment is rigid and monotonous. To some species this is not too much of a problem for they respond by spending more time resting and sleeping. To others, the neophilic species, it is extremely frustrating and they react in several ways which we have all seen at the zoo, even if we have not understood them.

The most obvious response is to perform rhythmic movements such as pacing up and down or walking in a circle or figure-of-eight path. Many develop other stereotype movements such as swaying, head bobbing or weaving. Some will spend so much time grooming and cleaning themselves that this may end in self-mutilation. This is particularly noticeable in monkeys and parrots.

Many try to relieve the boredom by reacting with the public or by playing with objects – even playing with their food. Some species pretend to stalk and 'kill' their food as they would do in the wild. Animals that normally prepare their food are not content to accept a ready-to-eat diet. Agoutis will conscientiously clean and peel their food and then eat the whole lot. Rodents will try, in vain, to bury their food in concrete.

More serious adaptations are an abnormal increase in the degree of reaction to normal stimuli, an increase in sexual activity or aggression and repeated regurgitation and ingestion of food.

In the wild, an animal's time is predominantly taken up with avoiding enemies, seeking food and procreation. These occupational necessities disappear in captivity. So an artificial life-cycle must be created and it must be adequate to break the monotony of life under captive conditions. If the environment is restricted and impoverished, then one can expect abnormality of behaviour, and of brain development in those born in that environment. Examples of poor quality environment are lack of companions with which to interact and play; lack of complexity – no trees, no vegetation and no variation of the territory – and lack of the facilities necessary to fulfil basic instincts and desires, such as digging, climbing and hunting.

Hand-reared animals may become anti-social to members of their own species. They may show increased offensive or defensive aggression, frigidity, or poor maternal instincts even though they seem adapted to the unbiological conditions of captivity. It has been clearly shown in experiments that rats raised in an impoverished environment show marked under-development of brain size, enzyme activity and learning ability.

Hand-reared. (The Daily Telegraph)

An animal's territory or home range in the wild is not determined by the animal's desire to control as big an area as possible. Several factors are involved. Availability of food is of prime importance and its ability to defend the area. Exercise is provided by the need to move about to gather food and to avoid danger. These factors also keep the animal busy and occupied. At other times they rest and sleep.

In the zoo where food is provided and danger removed, lack of exercise and boredom result. More important than size of enclosure is the quality and variety of the area, as well as the flight distance – the distance from danger at which the animal will turn and run away. Flight distance varies with each species and with each individual. Should the public be allowed within the individual's flight distance (i.e. too close) and the animal cannot hide away, it will be living in a state of tension.

Also important to social species is the structure of the family or group, which zoos rarely make adequate provision for.

So, having studied the problem carefully with the knowledge available at the present time we can conclude that some animals adapt to certain captive conditions while other species do not and, therefore, suffer and sometimes perish. Even if the zoo animal is bred in captivity the process of adaptation entails some suffering and we must decide whether that degree of suffering is sufficient for us to say that wild animals should not be held captive at all. There are species that can adapt and some that do not adapt at all, and within a species there are individuals that cannot tolerate captive conditions.

The philosophical and emotional view is more difficult to describe. I feel uneasy in the presence of a captive animal, even when I cannot say it is suffering. Even in the zoos thought to be the best, captivity cripples the animal just as urban dwelling often cripples human beings. The animal sitting in the enclosure is naked without its natural environment and our sense of wonder is absent.

Homo sapiens is a prisoner of his culture and environment. Therefore his view-point on captive animals will be narrow and limited unless he has had the good fortune to know the naturalness of an aboriginal people uninfluenced by western culture. For it should be remembered that mankind has a background of several million years of evolution and only ten thousand years of modern culture.

Those who have lived amongst the last few remaining aborigines can testify to a pleasant, easy life, for they work on average 20 hours per week. They are more lovable and at ease than civilized man, with no famines, few crimes and no H-bombs. Modern man has created a social structure that has taken on a life and momentum of its own and within which we are all captive and toiling. In our industrial society the things that get done are those conducive to economic growth. Lewis Mumford* has postulated: 'If

* *The Myth of the Machine* by Lewis Mumford, an American Philosopher and Commentator.

man had originally inhabited a world as blankly uniform as a high-rise housing development, as featureless as a parking lot, as destitute of life as an automatic factory, it is doubtful that he would have had sufficiently varied experience to retain images, mould a language or acquire ideas.' Indeed, young people raised in such a featureless environment and limited to a narrow range of life experiences are often crippled intellectually. Socially deprived, emotionally disturbed youths are a feature of our disintegrating societies. There is every reason to believe that the social ills at present afflicting society – vandalism, alcoholism, drug addiction – are closely related to, and symptoms of, a break down of our cultural pattern.

Plato says that men are not content with the simple life, 'they are inquisitive, ambitious, competitive and jealous. They soon tire of what they have and pine for what they have not. . . the result is the encroachment of

The animal sitting in the enclosure is naked without its natural environment and our sense of wonder is absent. (John Young)

one group upon the territory of another.' Certainly man defends his territory and is therefore restricted to some extent within it. According to Rousseau, the builder of the first fence was the founder of civilization. Man is a prisoner of his heredity and environment. Therefore his viewpoint on captive animals will be narrow and based on his own captive circumstances.

Ironically, apart from satisfying curiosity, another reason for keeping animals captive by either confinement or domestication is to preserve, however unnaturally, our proximity with nature, which in turn gives us some feeling of well-being or even happiness.

When Darwin first experienced the tropical rainforest he spoke of his astonishment and of a feeling of wonder that filled and elevated his mind. I believe that our ancient ancestry binds us to nature and the natural life. Recognizing and respecting that union is an essential part of our mental development, peace of mind and contentment. The natural world is the refuge of man's spirit. What is left of human instincts needs to be protected against becoming overwhelmed by culture and the modern environment, allowing human beings to live in harmony and peace, developing and growing towards their full potential. The fulfilment of these instincts is best accomplished through nature with awe and wonder. However, as we cannot return to the life of the hunter and gatherer, we must somehow control the machine created by our culture which is tearing apart the natural world we need.

As if any confirmation was needed, it occurred while I was wondering how I could explain my feelings. Horace, a free-living wild black bird, flew down on to the table in the garden a foot from my hand and turning his head aside he looked me in the eye. A feeling of happiness and peace spread throughout my body. It was followed by one of fulfilment and of belonging, without which I would be incomplete and lost. Horace is not a pet. True, we fed him for a week or so after his mother was killed and now we are friends. To keep him in a cage would be wrong. It would also prevent any feeling of fulfilment and belonging arising in me. For it would have disrupted the harmony of life and living by erecting an unnecessary barrier between the two parts. If man becomes separated from the natural world he will be like a cancer, growing in, feeding on and distorting the body and yet not part of it.

Mary Midgley

Keeping Species on Ice

Mary Midgley is a profession-al philosopher who became interested in animal behaviour from reading about it when she took time off from lecturing to bring up her children. After returning to work as a philoso-phy lecturer at the University of Newcastle-upon-Tyne she de-veloped this interest both theoretically, in the direction of attempting to understand better the relation between humans and other animals, and practi-cally, by discussing problems arising from the way in which animals ought to be treated. Her first book, *Beast and Man* (Methuen, 1980), dealt with the theoretical issues, and she has returned to them recently in *Evolution as a Religion* (Methuen, 1985). On the practical side she has written *Animals and Why They Matter* (Penguin, 1983). She lives in Newcastle, is married to Geoffrey Midgley (also a philo-sopher) and has three sons.

What do conservationists want to conserve? Are their true clients individual creatures, particular species or whole environments? Questions like this are so confusing that they can make people feel that the whole cause involved is somehow invalid. This is a mistake. We can in fact raise this kind of difficulty about every large-scale effort. Should social workers aim only at rescuing individuals, or should they instead help families, or communities? When we look at these cases, we probably see at once that there is no choice at all. Large and small groupings cannot be dealt with in isolation. They stand or fall together. Though sharp local conflicts can sometimes arise between them, their basic mutual interdependence goes much deeper. We normally take for granted the background where all groupings co-exist in a rough balance. We are scarcely conscious of it.

When the normal background starts to break up, however, things get much harder. New conflicts arise; existing ones become sharper. We can no longer rely on an underlying system which holds the various interests involved in some kind of loose balance. However much we may dislike thinking, we are forced at this point to start philosophizing, to work out principles on which the various interests can be reconciled or, where they cannot, priorities for deciding between them. If we are taking conservation seriously at all, we have already decided that the interests of species other than our own are important. (It does not matter for the moment whether this is because they matter for their own sake, or because their prospering is in itself important to man). In dealing with these various non-human interests we can confront, however, a wide variety of conflicts between different kinds of unit – species, genus, individual, habitat or total environment. We shall not find here, any more than in the human case, a single, simple principle which will resolve them neatly. But that does not mean we have to conclude, either about humans or animals, that thought is useless. Thought's 'business' is to sort out the different kinds of value which we can sensibly attribute to each interest.

When we start to wonder about the value which any special unit or grouping might possess, the most puzzling cases tend to be those in the middle of the range, such as the species. It is much easier to see what kind of value an individual has, because a great deal of our moral and political thinking has been devoted to it. And at the other end, the enclosing whole, the total environment, clearly has a special status in relation to its parts. It is more than the sum of them; it is, in fact, the condition on which their existence depends. But what is special about a species? What standing has it when its interests conflict with those of its individual members, or with those of a larger whole? These conflicts can be quite sharp. They arise with special force over the conservation of rare species in zoos, for eventual release.

This species-conservation is now sometimes put forward as the central and all-justifying aim of zoo-keeping. And when it works, it is indeed a triumph, a genuine piece of effective humaneness. Successes, however, are rare. The value of any scheme of this kind has to depend, not just on the value of the species to be saved – which is not easily assessed – but on the reasonable hope of restoring it in the end to its original niche.

Since what puts a species in danger in the first place is usually the destruction of its habitat, the zoos' holding operation is doomed, unless it is backed by effective local conservation. Good zoos know this, and do what they can for conservation propaganda. But the problem is so vast that it seems naïve to rely heavily on its ever being widely solved. If it is not, can the conserved species be kept in the air forever? If so, would it still be a species in the normal sense, and have the kind of value which species characteristically have? Or does that value depend on their playing their part in a larger system? If it probably cannot ever be re-established, does the remote possibility of returning it to a natural environment justify the special strains imposed on its present captive members for the sake of an uncertain and elusive future?

Dark Prospects

On a bad day, when one has been reading the scientific press and absorbing the usual reports of massive habitat-destruction, the re-establishment project begins to look rather like cryogenics – freezing people for eventual return to an improved and more hospitable world. This has two grave drawbacks. One is that the improvements needed for their return may never take place. The other is that, if they do take place, by that time the preserved specimen may be past benefiting from them. Indeed, the freezing process itself may already have proved fatal. 'Frozen' captive species face similar dangers. As is now being realized, the captive gene-pool is likely to be far too small. Are more specimens to be hastily caught from the wild, with the usual waste and disturbance which this involves? Or must the genes already available be somehow husbanded to take the strain? The horns of this dilemma currently impale mountain gorillas, Californian condors and many

Gorillas in the wild. (Ian Redmond)

more. No technical 'fix' is going to get rid of it. To maximize available variety, selective breeding considerations will have to take precedence over everything else in the social life of the zoo specimens. Fertile pairs cannot be allowed to continue breeding freely at will, lest they unbalance the gene-pool. Contraception will be needed, and whether it is done by segregation, by hormone treatment, by vasectomy or by death it will have socially disturbing consequences.

Again, where breeding is successful, there will simply be more animals than the zoo in question can afford to keep. Not all of them can be passed on to other zoos, so if their habitat is still unfit to receive them, they are at present (like other surplus animals in zoos) either quietly killed or – still more disturbingly – passed on to research institutions for experimentation. In short, as Jeremy Cherfas puts it, we shall all have to 'realize that, if animals are to be preserved in captivity, individuals are subjugate to the species.'*

In these species, then, the welfare of existing animals is supposed to give way systematically, not just to human interests, but also to the surmized future interests of their own possible remote descendants. If this is to be justified, the prospects of success had better be good. Sometimes indeed they are so. The new Tsavo Rhino Sanctuary in Kenya is an impressive case. Very often, however, the hopes are both distant and dubious; the captivity must at best be a long one. A further Catch-22 situation then adds itself to the snags already listed. Captive creatures inevitably become, to some extent, adapted to captivity. The more technological miracles are performed on them, the more certain this must be, because there will be steady selection for the ability to tolerate, or even enjoy, manhandling and the general presence of people, and to accept human restrictions on their social life. In the wild, however, these qualities could be disastrous. As Sanford Friedman points out, prolonged species-conservation faces zoos with a painful choice:

> After all, what is a species? If a zoo animal looks like a Siberian tiger, is it?. . . Should our breeding programs be directed towards preserving the genetic diversity present in the wild population, or towards maintaining individual animals suited to captivity? The latter provides the greatest probability of long-term survival in captivity, but may result in genetic changes that cannot be reversed and that will restrict our future options, including release into the wild.†

In short, serious conservation of captive species for re-establishment is an extremely difficult and exacting business. While not impossible, it has requirements which are very hard to combine with the other aims of zoo-keeping. It is not an automatic spin-off from normal zoo practice, but a demanding occupation on its own. Most zoos are quite unable to contribute

* 'Breeding to Death' (*The Guardian*, Futures, 1 November 1984)

† *International Zoo News* March/April 1985.

effectively to it, and it cannot properly be used as a general answer to criticisms of zoo-keeping.

Dependence and Alienation

Public discussions of conservation-by-captivity projects are beginning to show some awareness of these difficulties. However, the simplicity of the initial idea was so attractive that critical response has only gradually emerged. The popular press, of course, still tends to be euphoric, in the manner of the *Daily Express* report on release-into-the-wild projects (28 June 1984), which remarked that Longleat Safari Park had a 'tiger booked for Zambia soon. Africa has no tigers in the wild.' Fortunately, no responsible body is now likely to set about exporting tigers to remedy this kind of 'deficiency'. In scientific papers, naturally, things are better, but even there the tone sometimes seems unduly optimistic. For scientists, the chief enemy of realism is faith in the technical 'fix'. Authors mention the difficulties of captive breeding, but they tend then to move smoothly on to the miracles of modern science by which, it is hoped, these hiccups in progress can be overcome.

These miracles are chiefly, at present, techniques for freezing and replicating sperm, ova and embryos. The main obstacles to release-into-the-wild do not, however, concern this phase of life at all. They arise after birth. They are social and developmental. They spring partly from the captive creatures' inevitable deep addiction to a dependent life-style, which leaves them bewildered by the trauma of release, and partly from the refusal of local members of the same species to make room for them in the release area. (If there are no local members of the same species, other creatures are likely to have occupied their niche and things are no better). These problems – which are of course sharpest in the case of advanced social creatures – are by now well known and documented by those who have attempted the project.

Thus Stella Brewer, who, after long experience of African wild-life, devoted herself to attempting the rehabilitation and release of a few young chimps, has reported the almost crushing difficulties of the task.* Yet these were wild-born apes, which had only had a brief experience of captivity. They had not been born in an atmosphere of anaesthetics and disinfectant, nor lived for years in the smell of people, plastics and cars. Joy Adamson has described similar difficulties in releasing Elsa. Her eventual brief success ought not to obscure the grave drawbacks to the whole idea which emerge from her story. Individual creatures bred in dependence may welcome a wider range, but they do not at all want to be 'released' – that is, deserted and abandoned, any more than those already there want to receive them. We should not ourselves like to be dropped without explanation in the middle of

---

* *The Forest Dwellers* (Collins, 1978).

the jungle, although our ancestors, as much as those of the apes, developed there and adapted to it.

For this kind of difficulty, technical 'fixes' are no help. The endless demanding rehabilitation work which is needed is not technical at all. It is personal and emotional and what it can possibly achieve is sharply limited. Yet projects like this still seem to be lightly undertaken. A Dutch vet was hired to take a year-old gorilla, called Julia, bought from an animal-dealer in Belgium, 'back' to the Gambia, for release in the wild. (Marian Mensink, *New Scientist*, 19 June 1986). There are, of course, no gorillas in the Gambia and those sending the ape did not originally even know whether she was a lowland or a mountain gorilla. Discovering she was of the lowland variety they sent her to the Abuko Nature Reserve, to join some young chimps who were being trained for release. The climate was wrong (hot and dry), the terrain was wrong, but worst of all the species was wrong, and for that there is no remedy:

> Julia had many problems. It had been hard to separate her from her human foster-parents. She had to cope with new people, new foods, a new climate. . . .She became obviously neurotic – hiding under blankets, continually troubled. She appeared a sad, pathetic, disorientated little being. . . .It is true there were chimps. But chimps are chimps; they are not gorillas. Although, as her tutor, I could pretend to be a gorilla, I was a very poor substitute for the real thing.

Julia is still in captivity. The author also describes various other recent attempts to introduce chimps by force into a wild African habitat, against both their own grain and that of the existing populations, and she reasonably asks whether this money could not be better spent directly on conserving the forest? Surely she is right. The real threat to these populations is economic and political. Unless the forest can be saved from the loggers and ranchers, the apes are doomed in any case. Apart from this major threat, their chief minor danger is that of poachers and trappers, whose market comes partly from zoos and other bodies anxious to possess these rare creatures. From this end too, change is surely needed. Zoos ought not to be buying them. Animal dealers ought not to be in a position to sell a creature like Julia at all. Instead, they should be subject to a swingeing fine for having bought her in the first place.

There is no substitute for the wild. With rare exceptions, all the species of a habitat will normally be saved or lost together. Lifeboats that merely offer to save one specially spectacular creature on its own are of little use.

The Lure of the Technical Fix
Today, people evidently find this point hard to see. Their difficulty about it relates, perhaps, to a similar difficulty about modern medicine. Preventive measures are seen as less exciting than cures. This quirk of taste is linked with a habitual bold confidence that, if we neglect prevention, cures will still come in at the last moment to save us. The resultant unwillingness to take prevention seriously has something to do with the fact that preventive

measures tend to force us to deal with obviously complex, messy problems of organizing human life, whereas cures, at least when viewed from a sufficiently rosy distance, seem to call only for a simple technical fix. This bizarre notion can be seen at work in another interesting article by Jeremy Cherfas – normally a very shrewd and responsible scientific journalist – about the increasing shortage of chimpanzees for research (*New Scientist* 27 March 1986.) Cherfas points out that current research demands 180 chimpanzees a year in the USA. Few chimps are available and it is hard to increase the number:

> Although there are about 1500 chimpanzees in captivity, about 300 in zoos and the rest in research establishments, they are not breeding well, especially in zoos. A basic problem that excludes many animals from breeding programmes is hepatitis, especially non-A and non-B hepatitis. Although it does not make the animals sick, it raises unknown risks for research programmes, and animals that have been exposed to it are not used in breeding for fear that they will infect others.

On top of this, very simple financial considerations have distorted the sexual development and breeding behaviour of most of the remaining healthy animals:

> If a baby chimp is removed from its mother soon after birth, the mother can be mated again and will produce another 10,000-dollar baby more quickly. . .the baby snatched like this, while apparently healthy enough, almost inevitably develops aberrant social and sexual behaviour, so that when it is mature it is unlikely to breed successfully. In 1980 the breeding population consisted of 145 females and 63 males; of these only seventeen females and four males were themselves born in captivity.

The main solution proposed is a dedicated breeding colony, in which infants would be left much longer with their mothers. As planned, this would produce thirty chimpanzees a year. Cherfas remarks: 'The problem is that thirty animals is too few by about 150. Where is the shortfall to come from?'

It seems plain at this point that the wrong end of the equation is being tackled. What is needed is that scientists should agree on a way of reducing their demand. Priorities must be weighed, as with any other scarce resource, and a discipline accepted. This is so even if one considers no other interest at all except that of science itself. Have present scientists no duty to future ones? If science really needs chimpanzees, it must preserve the species, instead of working, as it evidently has been doing, to hasten their extinction. By drawing all those breeding individuals from the wild, it has already encouraged the trappers and put strain on the remaining stocks. (When such an individual is captured as an infant, the trappers must normally kill its whole family to get it. In addition about half such infants die before reaching the market). The geese that lay these golden eggs are getting rare. At some point the lust for gold will have to be restrained, and there is no point in putting that moment off till things get even harder.

This, however, is not what Cherfas advises. His first proposal is that the 'behavioural incompetence' which prevents breeding might be reversed by suitable 'training and therapy'. Since no profession of experienced 'chimp-shrinks' exists, there is no evidence to support this hope. After this, accordingly, comes the expected dive for consolation into the embryological laboratory, but this time with a rather unusual twist:

> One approach that has not yet been attempted is surrogate motherhood. . .Surrogacy could also be tried across species. . .existing techniques would allow a fertilized chimpanzee egg to be implanted into a very closely related, and more plentiful species, say *Homo sapiens*. The most impressive of such techniques would wrap a chimpanzee inner cell mass in the emptied blastocyst of a human zygote; the blastocyst – the outer layer of the developing embryo – forms a perfectly compatible human embryo, while the inner cell mass develops into a chimpanzee.

Is 'bizarre' too strong a word for this idea? How are the human surrogate mothers to be found? But on top of its other strange features, it is totally irrelevant to the need it is supposed to meet. That need was (you will remember) to produce chimps which have had a normal chimpanzee mothering – which have not been distorted from their species-specific development, and which have been kept free from contact with human diseases such as hepatitis. The euphoria associated with new technology seems to have driven this aim right out of the author's head. His proposal, even if it could be carried out, seems adapted only to produce more Frankenstein's monsters – animals who, like Julia, are unable to live the life proper to their own species, and are equally incapable of joining any other. Such maimed creatures often cannot breed or rear young. Many already exist in this predicament, experimental chimps being prominent among them, since their way of life depends entirely on the flow of research money, which bears no relation at all to their social requirements.

These creatures are our responsibility. It has been entirely natural for people to hope that they might be happily disposed of by sending them to reinforce failing populations in the wild, thus killing two birds with one stone. It is distressing to find that this scheme does not necessarily work, any better than well-meant attempts to rehabilitate depressed townspeople by settling them on the land. For many of the captive creatures, other solutions must be found. In the case of the American chimps, there is Jane Goodall's current Chimpanzoo project for better planned, larger and more spacious zoo colonies. Wildlife parks may do a similar service for other species of captive laboratory animals.

For failing wild populations, we shall need other remedies, which must take account of the factors causing them to fail in the first place. On one point, however, arguments from both angles firmly converge. We need to stop producing these socially deformed animals. Interspecies surrogacy would be liable to produce them. It should therefore be viewed with great suspicion, however impressive its technology may be.

Sorts of Value

Thinking about the predicament of these unlucky animals can, however, help us to cast some light on the puzzling question we started from – that concerning the special kind of value which attaches to a species.

What confuses us is that this value has at least two different elements. There are, so to speak, two kinds of light here, cast from different sources. From the individual angle, the species provides (as we have just noticed) an irreplaceable context for proper growth, a community within which the life of a social animal can be properly articulated. This need is crucial. Creatures fostered by another species do not represent an exception to it. They are not emancipated from the bonds of species. In so far as they make out at all, they do so by behaving as if they belonged to the same species as those around them. But their own natural constitution sets limits to this possibility. Where these barriers arise, creatures must remain alien and frustrated. They cannot pass on, with impartial judiciousness, to interact with some other group instead. This importance of species-membership for individual life has been somewhat obscured to us lately by the comparison of 'speciesism' with racism – a comparison which has a good point so far as 'speciesism' simply means species-vanity or species-imperialism, but which is misleading if it is taken to dismiss all attachments to one's species as a mere discreditable prejudice. No animal is just an abstract animal-as-such. All, if they are social, need their own special community.

Of course this is not all they need. They need their whole appropriate background, their habitat. This brings us to the other end of the value-spectrum – the angle of the whole. From this point of view, each species is a component part, one of those which contribute to the overall character of the ecosystem. No doubt some are less essential to this character than others, and at any given time, some may be predominantly destructive. But this situation is harder to be sure of than we tend to think, and we are always being caught out when we conclude that something ought to be eliminated. In any case, the whole depends in general on its parts in the simple sense that it has no existence without them.

It is one of the privileges of human beings that they are capable, in some degree, of appreciating both these kinds of value. To articulate them fully, we would need to connect them with other values in a way which our culture already shadows out for us to some extent, and which we can ourselves develop more fully. The value of the whole has been celebrated in many ways, ways which tend in general to be religious, though of course not necessarily Christian or even theist. The value of an individual sentient life has also been worked out, for western culture, more in moral and political terms than in religious ones. Since it has been invoked in the course of political struggles against oppression within human communities, it has often been linked explicitly with human species-membership ('the rights of man') and has been seen as flowing from a kind of rationality which was supposed to be exclusively human.

At the same time, however, there has grown up a general humaneness, a sense of fellowship, a compassion and respect for sentient life as such, which makes natural an extension of this kind of regard to non-human individuals. This humaneness does appear to be central to the morality we actually accept today. Both these kinds of consideration converge to make us deem species worthy of preservation, and though the reasons they offer are distinct, there is no general conflict between them. Where local conflicts

The early morning fox in the New Forest, England. (Eric Ashby)

arise, we must, then, arbitrate them on their merits.

I do not see any general reason in our value-system for ruling that individuals ought, in general, to be 'subjugate to their species', and I do not think that is what Jeremy Cherfas was suggesting. No doubt there can be occasions when they must be sacrificed for it and that could occur even in the case of human beings. But we need to be very careful not to accept any such simplifying principle wholesale. As usual in such cases, we should try to prevent the conflicts which call for the sacrifice from arising in the future. If habitats really are lost, their denizens cannot for ever be preserved behind bars. Even while they are preserved, and even for the limited purposes of science, they will quickly cease to be proper, typical specimens of their original kind.

However, the reasons why we value species go far beyond those limited scientific purposes. Science itself is not just an information-grubbing device or a hobby for eccentrics; it is the admiring study of the world around us. It matters because that world itself is wonderful and excellent. Species, while they remain in that context, contribute to its glory and have each their own irreplaceable value as a part of it. Taken away from it, they tend, like seaweed brought home from a holiday, to lose their splendour, dry up, wither and finally die. Zoos have, even with the best will in the world, only a limited power to delay this process, and we ought not to deceive ourselves about it by putting a disproportionate trust in them.

Whales

Sea haunting giant
Music maker of Oceans
Hidden harmless hunted Hercules
Wave washed wanderer
Water cloaked Emperor
Liberty loving leviathan
Gracious God given colossus
Oh that I could dream a dream
as big as thou.

Spike Milligan

Hout Bay, South Africa
17 October 1983

Richard Adams

Some Thoughts on Animals in Religious Imagery

R ichard Adams, born in 1920, studied Modern History at Worcester College, Oxford, and after military service during the Second World War joined the Civil Service. Between 1966 and 1967 he wrote the now famous *Watership Down* based on a story he invented to amuse his two young daughters during a long car journey. The book was published in 1972 and won the Carnegie Medal and *The Guardian* award for children's fiction. In 1974 he retired from the Civil Service as an Assistant Secretary at the Department of the Environment to devote his time to writing. There followed *Shardik* (Penguin, 1976), *Nature Day and Night* (with Max Hooper) (Penguin, 1980), *The Plague Dogs* (Penguin, 1978), *The Girl in a Swing* (Penguin, 1981), *The Iron Wolf* (Penguin, 1982), *Voyage Through the Antarctic* (with Ronald Lockley) (A. Lane, 1982), *Maia* (Viking, 1984), *The Bureaucats* (Viking Kestrel, 1985), and *A Nature Diary* (Viking, 1985). He was President of the RSPCA from 1980 to 1982.

It is the literal truth that there is scarcely an animal in the world that has not been, at some time and by some group or society, worshipped. It is also true that animals and animal imagery have been integral to every religion practised in the world – including Christianity – from the earliest times to the present day.

Man's first gropings towards notions of the divine, his desire to approach and feel himself to be on some kind of terms with it, to propitiate it, to assimilate its spiritual power and thus derive confidence and a sense of being protected, can be traced back to the time, a million years ago, when we were scarcely more than animals ourselves. Augusta and Burin, in their remarkable book on Prehistoric Man, have shown that the Neanderthalers observed crude ceremonial burial customs. (That is, they did not suppose themselves to be merely disposing of a body.) Among the most fascinating and inscrutable of primitive man's cults is that of the cave bears. Like man, the great bears also frequented caves. In certain eastern European caves, collections have been found of numerous bear skulls, evidently assembled and preserved from magical and possibly devotional motives. (Even if the bears had been killed to eat or for their skins, it could have served no merely utilitarian purpose to collect and arrange the skulls.) It must have been both difficult and dangerous, with the resources available to the cave men, to hunt and kill these bears, and it seems probable that the hunting itself may have constituted part of the cult. By applying the necessary cunning, skill and courage, the cave men probably felt that they could assimilate the strength, endurance and other qualities of the bear. We do not know whether they actually accorded it anything which we today would call worship, but it seems clear, on the evidence of the skull collections, that by attaching special significance to the bear they regarded it, in some indistinct but valid respect, as having a transcendental quality: in short, as partaking of the divine.

The narrative culture of primitive people, as we know from modern surviving examples, largely deals – spontaneously, of course, not deliberately – with notions of how this or that phenomenon came to be; attempts to explain otherwise inexplicable natural marvels. These 'explanations' often take the form of tales about the animals and birds among whom such men live and with whom they feel themselves to share the world on more-or-less equal terms. Tales about animals – explanations of the divine order in terms of the adventures of animals and their dealings with gods or with each other – form the bedrock of narrative folk lore of the most primitive peoples known to us.

For example, F. H. Lee's anthology *Folk Tales of All Nations* (Harrap, 1931) includes the following titles (appended by him, of course) of the Australian aborigine stories: 'The Wonderful Lizard'; 'How the Selfish Goannas Lost Their Wives'; 'The Mischievous Crow'; 'Dinewan the Emu'; 'Goolahwilleel, the Topknot Pigeons'; 'Wayambeh the Turtle'; 'Gooloo the Magpie'; 'Weedah the Mocking Bird'. Similarly, from among the tales of the Hottentots, Lee selected 'The Jackal's Bride'; and 'The Dove and the Heron', while from the Congo he took 'The Cat and the Rat'; 'The Jackal and the Drought' and 'The Rabbit and the Crocodile'. Many other examples could be given from the folk-tales of the Esquimaux, the Pueblo Indians, the Tibetans, the tribesmen of Malaya, etc. The point of significance is that among primitive people, self-conscious narrative first emerges in the form of *animal* tales.

It has been said that anthropomorphic fantasy is the oldest form of social satire. 'Satire', however, is too sophisticated and precise a term for these tales. Certainly they attribute human motives and human behaviour to animals, but less with the idea of deriding people in their own society than of explaining that society – or explaining some aspect of the nature of the world. 'We know it was thus,' says the narrator, 'because the tale says it was thus,' or 'because the ancestors told us.' In the same way, a small child will often narrate his own fantasy and maintain that it is true, for he does not yet understand, in adult terms, the meanings of 'true' and 'false', and anyway he perceives intuitively that, for stories, the rules are different.

From the Polynesian Islands – as recounted by Joseph Campbell in *The Masks of God* (Penguin, 1983) – comes the tale of Te Tuna, Maui and Hina. This is of considerable interest, since it constitutes not only a typical example of a 'How the So-and-So Came About' tale, but also what must surely be a very old instance of a universal type of story; of a divine gift bestowed upon mankind as the result of a numinous and god-like death. The protagonist, sure enough, is an animal. Here, too, we shall see exemplified the ingredient of paradox which forms part of so much of man's religious animal imagery. The terrible, the fierce, the jealous, the meek and the generous are conjoined; the light and the darkness are, in some incomprehensible manner, united. This paradox has always formed an integral part of religious thought, and for that very reason is continually implicit in the animal imagery used as a means of religious expression.

Te Tuna was the most feared creature in the world; the giant eel of the Polynesian ocean. He lived in a coral palace below the waves, and at one time his consort was Hina, a beautiful girl who may be more-or-less equated with Aphrodite (or any fertility goddess). However, Hina grew weary of Te Tuna, that ferocious, phallic power, and devised a pretext to steal away from him (for she would have been afraid to leave him openly) and go back to the world above the sea. Having returned, she offered herself as a lover to Maui, the folk-hero of the Polynesian and Maori peoples. (Maui, magician, hero, thief, lover and trickster, is a kind of blend of Hercules, Hermes, Prometheus, Odysseus and Robin Hood. His deeds include exploits similar to some of those of each of these characters.) Maui and Hina thereupon began living together on one of the islands.

Te Tuna, learning of this, set out with his eel-warriors to destroy Maui. Maui, however, defeated Te Tuna and killed his warriors by a magical drying-up of the lagoon as they were swimming towards him. Te Tuna himself he spared, and took him home to his hut. After a time, however, Te Tuna said that they must have a duel to the death. This he began by entering into Maui's body and thus trying to destroy him, but eventually he was forced to reappear, unsuccessful. Maui then entered the giant eel's body and destroyed *him*. He cut off the head and buried it outside his hut. Some weeks or months later a tree began to grow from the buried head. Maui's mother, a magical wise woman, told him that he now had a divine duty to tend and propagate the tree. This is how the coconut, the staple of the South Sea islands' economy, was bestowed upon Polynesia.

To examine ancient Egyptian religion and its symbolism of animals is to come upon a cult – relatively recent, of course, dating from no more than a few thousand years ago which strikes us today, from the pictorial evidence, as mysterious, daunting, esoteric and even if beneficent, nevertheless somewhat sinister. Ancient Egyptian religion was based, quite consciously, upon the concept of a god's sacred death and resurrection; and this was connected with the fertility of the crops. Here is the religion of an agrarian people, whose economy differed *in kind* from that of primitive man, of the Australian aborigines and of the Esquimaux, for all these were hunters. The death and sacred gift of Te Tuna were thought of by the Polynesians (who reap no harvest), as unique, single occurrences; they did not recur. Death and resurrection in ancient Egypt, however, were cyclical, and related – how consciously we do not know – to the flooding of the Nile. The performance of certain religious practices are thought to have been considered essential to ensuring that the Nile did duly flood. Religion was also connected, of course, both with human fertility and with life beyond death. There are few modern stories and imaginative fantasies about ancient Egypt, but one well worth reading is William Golding's novella *The Scorpion God* (Faber, 1973).

The ancient Egyptian pantheon was made up of a rather fearsome array of animal gods and goddesses. It is an interesting feature that, unlike their predecessors the cave bears and the divine animals of primitive people, they had human limbs and bodies; while unlike their successors, the gods of Greece and Rome, they had animals' heads (sometimes the reverse). Perhaps, therefore, we can here discern a kind of imagic stepping-stone, in religious imaginative portrayal, between the all-animal and the all-human. An excellent book – lavishly illustrated – for the ordinary reader is *Egypt* by Claudio Barocas, in the 'Monuments of Civilization' series. Here is the terrible Sphinx, with her woman's head and lion's body, destroyer of those who cannot answer her riddle. (Incidentally, a penetrating and disturbing sonnet about the Sphinx, by W. H. Auden, is worth seeking out.) On the wall of a Karnak chapel the god Horus, with falcon's head, embraces King Sesostris I. Horus and his companion Thoth – who has the head of an ibis – pour out the stream of life on Queen Hatshepsut. The goddess Sekhmet, with a lion's head, protects King Seti I. In one wall-painting, in the tomb of Sennadem at Deir-el-Medinet, the dog-headed god Anubis stoops over the dead king to embalm him. In another, a cat (with rabbit's ears) slashes Apopus, serpent-god of the underworld, with a kind of crimson scimitar. 'Almost every god,' says Claudio Barocas, 'could be represented by a certain animal, without that animal being considered exactly an incarnation of the god. This characteristic. . . must certainly have very ancient roots. We might speculate on. . . animal cults, or a certain type of totemism. . . a relationship to sacred animals. Very likely we attach more importance to the presence of such animals than did the ancient Egyptians themselves.'

As is widely known, the Minoan civilization of ancient Crete, which flourished during the second millennium BC, associated the bull with its entire culture and religion. Here is as clear an example as can well be found of the natural association with religion of an animal of outstanding beauty, strength and virility. It is clear from Minoan mural paintings that there existed some cult of the bull which involved young men and women in the no doubt dangerous sport or ritual of performing acrobatic somersaults and the like on a bull's horns and back. Mary Renault, in her imaginative romance *The King Must Die* (New English Library, 1970) – which narrates what might have been the historical truth behind the legend of Theseus – suggests that the 'bull-dancers' may have been boys and girls force-levied from subject states of the Minoan empire and dedicated to the performance of the bull-cult. However this may be, the legend of the Minotaur – a monster, half-man and half-bull – who killed and devoured his human tribute in the labyrinth, suggests the terror and hatred inspired by the bull-cult among other Mediterranean peoples subject to the Minoans. Two interesting features of the Minoan religion seem to be, first, that the bull itself does not appear to have been actually worshipped, but rather to have been a kind of divine adjunct of the worship of Minos, a sacred king and deified human being and, second, that the Minotaur, half-animal and half-human, was regarded as horrifying and disgusting – the result of an unnatural union – as the Egyptian animal-headed gods were not.

The civilization of ancient Greece incorporated a peaceful fusion of many

The goat – a potent religious symbol in ancient Greece. (Bill Travers)

legends and religions from all over the Mediterranean. There was no organized priestly class, no orthodox doctrine and, indeed, no consistency in the myths and legends. ('Now some say that after this. . .Others again maintain that. . .') But one thing is clear, despite the continuance of reverence for Pan, the goat-footed god of wild places, and the dread which they inspire (Panic fear), the 'official' gods and goddesses of ancient Greece – the Olympian Twelve (of which Pan was not one) – were imagined and represented as human beings. Magic and immortal they certainly were, and also capricious and amoral; but they themselves had no physical animal nature. However – and this is significant – their worship, as it were, *retained* birds and animals; which is as much as to say that their worshippers retained the birds and animals in what we may call their devotional imagination. Thus Zeus, snatched away at birth by his mother, Rhea, from his murderous father Cronus, was hidden in a cave on Mount Aegaeon and suckled by a goat. Having grown to maturity, overthrown Cronus and become omnipotent, (and the goat, in due time, having died), Zeus thereafter wore its skin in token of gratitude, and is accordingly styled 'Lord of the Aegis'. ('Aegis' means a goat-skin.) The goat, of course, was a creature of basic economic importance to the ancient Greeks. The eagle, also, was sacred to Zeus – a royal symbol requiring no explanation. Zeus, supreme on high, was all-seeing.

Animals and birds, therefore, while no longer divine in themselves, became divine *attributes*. In other words, despite the growing sophistication of the human intellect, the human psyche remained unable to apotheosize or worship without the imagery, beauty and stimulus which the animals and birds provided.

To Hera, the wife of Zeus, the peacock was an attribute; to Pallas Athena, the owl. This owl of Athena has in fact proved remarkably durable in the human psyche, for to this day he appears in nursery tales as a generic figure of wisdom, (the birds' schoolmaster, etc.) with his spectacles and mortarboard. Pooh's 'Wol' is directly descended from Pallas Athena's. Artemis, the virgin huntress, was drawn in her chariot by four golden stags. Hounds, too, were sacred to her. Frazer, in *The Golden Bough* (Macmillan, 1980), tells how, during her annual festival at Nemi in the Alban Hills of Italy, hunting dogs were adorned with crowns and wild beasts might not be hunted. Aphrodite, as a love-goddess with counterparts in the Orient, (Ashtaroth, Ishtar and other fertility goddesses), had several birds and animal attributes; sparrows, doves, swans, swallows and hares. The temple of Aphrodite at Corinth included sacred prostitutes, who were equated with the white doves also kept there. The tortoise was held sacred to Hermes, for one of his divine gifts to mankind had been the lyre and its music, which he devised by fastening taut strings across the shell of a tortoise he found at the entrance of his cave on Mount Cyllene in Arcadia. Poseidon, the sea-god, also conferred a divine gift on humanity; namely, the horse, which he created in the course of a dispute with Pallas Athena about the siting of Athens: and it was Poseidon, so the Greeks believed, who first taught the art of managing horses by the bridle (the ancients had neither saddles nor stirrups) and also originated horse races. His own chariot, indeed, with its 'white horses', was plain to be seen in the waves; and to this day we still call rough waves 'white horses'. Dionysus, whose cult originated in the Orient but who was 'adopted' into the Olympian Twelve as the son of Zeus and Semele, (daughter of Cadmus, King of Thebes), was a god of wine, orgiastic frenzy and trance-induced prophecy. He was associated with many attributive animals, notably leopards, lynxes and asses, as well as dolphins and serpents.

The serpent as a symbol in religious imagination is virtually universal and has in fact formed the subject of more than one book. We have already met Te Tuna, the giant eel, consort of the beautiful Hina; and we can pick him up again on the other side of the world by reading in Genesis of the serpent who beguiled the beautiful Eve. A discussion of the relationship between the two myths, as exemplifying the difference between the Polynesian and the ancient Judaic attitude towards sexuality, is included in Joseph Campbell's *The Masks of God* (Penguin, 1983). The divine quest upon which Pallas Athena sent Perseus was to bring her the head of Medusa, the serpent-haired Gorgon whose gaze turned people to stone. Having acquired the head, the goddess thereafter wore it in the centre of her shield. An interesting feature of this legend is that by emphasizing the paradox of the serpent it symbolizes the paradox at the heart of all religious mysticism. The toxin generates the anti-toxin – a scientific medical fact. The serpent is deadly: the serpent is the source of healing. Moses held up the brazen serpent to the Israelites in the desert, '. . . and it came to pass, that if a serpent had bitten any man, when he beheld the serpent of brass, he lived.' (Numbers XX1,9.) The concept of the mystical serpent, destroyer and preserver, may be equated with the concept of Light and Darkness, of Life and Death as eternally complementary. It has remained a potent image in the modern imagination. Coleridge's Ancient Mariner, in the moment when he blessed the water-snakes unaware, was able once more to pray and was released from the curse incurred by shooting the albatross. Readers of Thomas Hardy will recall the episode in *The Return of the Native*, when Mrs Yeobright is successfully treated for an adder's bite by the traditional method of killing other adders, frying them and applying to the wound the oil so produced. The badge of the Royal Army Medical Corps is a serpent twined about the healing staff of Hermes, (known to the Army as 'the worm climbing up a greasy pole').

Animal symbolism and imagery abound throughout the Bible. Since the Old Testament concerns the history and religious thought of a pastoral and agrarian people, it is natural that much of its imagery should derive from creatures familiar in the daily life of the highly moralistic society of Israel and Judah. (In both Egyptian and ancient Greek religion, the major preoccupation – as it seems to us today – was with the divine rather than the moral. It is to the genius of the Jews that we owe our own conception of

God with animals. (The British Library)

religion as a matter of humane morality as much as of mystic reverence for the numinous.) It is in the poetic rather than the historical books of the Old Testament that animal imagery appears most movingly. A favourite ploy of the writers of the Psalms, for instance, is to illustrate God's fatherly providence through the image of some animal or bird and its natural way of life. 'Yea, the sparrow hath found her an house, and the swallow a nest where she may lay her young; even thine altars, O Lord of Hosts, my King and my God.' (Psalm 84.) Plainly, the poet had watched these birds flying and nesting about the great temple at Jerusalem, the praise of which is the subject of the psalm. He wanted to present it as the exemplar of security and of the stability of family life sustained and blessed by a benevolent God; and to this end he used the birds as symbols of the temple's frequenters and devotees. (I have myself been moved to see swallows flying in and out above the stage at Glyndebourne, untroubled by Don Giovanni singing below.)

The author of the 91st Psalm, wishing to illustrate the invulnerability of the righteous man protected by God, says, 'Thou shalt tread upon the lion and adder: the young lion and the dragon shalt thou trample under thy feet.' (In this context, according to William Smith's *Dictionary of the Bible*, 1863, 'dragon' simply means a poisonous snake.)

The 104th Psalm could almost be quoted *in extenso*, but I particularly like verse eighteen: 'The high hills are a refuge for the wild goats; and the rocks for the conies.' (That is as much as to say that they, like ourselves, are retainers of God and form part of the divine order.) The latter animal, again according to William Smith, is *Hyrax syriacus* (*Procavia capensis*), a ruminant somewhat resembling a marmot and a little smaller than a cat. (Is it not, by the way, somewhat odd that cats remain unmentioned from one end of the Bible to the other, for surely the ancient Jews must have had domesticated cats in order to keep down rats and mice?)

Dogs, of course – like many other animals of a pastoral economy, e.g. asses, sheep and goats – occur frequently: sometimes as watchdogs ('His watchmen are blind...they are all dumb dogs, they cannot bark.' Isaiah LVI,10), sometimes as sheep-dogs ('...whose fathers I would have disdained to have set with the dogs of my flock.' Job XXX,1), and sometimes, rather surprisingly, simply as companion animals. (See *The Book of Tobit*, in which the dog's accompanying of Tobias on his journey is emphasized, though the animal plays no part of importance in the story.) Usually, however, – as one would expect from writers of the Orient – dogs appear as the unclean 'pie-ards', the feral and masterless carrion and refuse-devourers which have hung about villages in the Holy Land time out of mind. (I remember them vividly from days of war service in Palestine.) Jesus, like every person of his time, was familiar with these pie-ards, and used the image to symbolize the degradation of poor Lazarus. '...moreover the dogs came and licked his sores.' (Luke XVI,21.)

Jesus's bird and animal imagery, though always vivid and memorable, is augmentative and illustrative – down to earth – rather than poetic. Its quality is authentic and graphic, and its purpose simply to strike home readily to the sort of audiences whom he addressed. Wishing to stress his point that the grain of mustard seed became a great tree, he says '... and the fowls of the air lodged in the branches of it.' (Luke XIII,19.) The kind-hearted, generous Samaritan, finding the wounded traveller, '... set him on his own beast' (Luke X,34.) He himself then walked, one infers. The Lord will divide the nations '. . .as a shepherd divideth his sheep from the goats.' (Matthew XXV,32.) The disciples are sent forth '. . .as sheep in the midst of wolves: be ye therefore wise' (the New English Bible has 'wary') 'as serpents and harmless (or 'innocent') as doves.' (Matthew X,16.) The Pharisees are asked the deadly rhetorical question, 'Which of you shall have an ass or an ox fallen into a pit, and will not straightway pull him out on the sabbath day?' (Luke XIV,5.) It is interesting that Our Lord made no use at all of highly-charged, magical animal imagery – lions, dragons or such-like mythical beasts. (The Book of Revelation, by contrast, includes eleven allusions to dragons.)

I suppose not many people read Revelation nowadays. It is an overwhelming book, unlike anything else in the Bible and, indeed, unlike anything else in the heritage of Western literature. As an imagic vision of Doomsday and Judgement it fairly knocks you flat with angels, trumpets, fire, smoke, thunder and lightning, plague, famine, beasts with seven heads and ten horns, women with the wings of eagles, mighty voices from heaven, earthquakes, piles of dead bodies littering the streets and goodness knows what else besides. Its animal imagery recalls nothing so much as the mythical dragons (properly called 'kylins') of China, or the chindits of Burma. There never were such beasts. They come either from heaven or from hell; and that is the whole point of them. It is all a mystical evocation of Apocalypse.

The writer is describing the transcendental and incomprehensible; yet in imagery which the human reader can visualize. (He or she can try, anyway.) 'The beast which I saw was like unto a leopard, and his feet were as the feet of a bear, and his mouth as the mouth of a lion: and the dragon gave him his power. . .' (XIII,2.) It is from Revelation that the church (and people in general) have derived much of our traditional and commonly accepted animal imagery and symbolism in regard to the Christian religion. While it was, of course, John the Baptist who first equated Christ with the Lamb of God, the sacrificial lamb of the Passover (John I,29 and 36), in Revelation this image occurs no fewer than twenty-six times. Again, from Revelation is derived the idea (though probably the writer meant something else) that the four evangelists are to be symbolized respectively as a lion, a calf (though he is nearly always depicted as a bull: archetypically more acceptable), a flying eagle and a beast with 'a face as a man'. (IV,7.) The four horsemen of the Apocalypse, also, are first found in Revelation, and very terrible they are in context. (VI, 2-8.) The four horses – white, red, black and 'pale' – are generally taken to represent War, Famine, Pestilence and Death, though personally I could never, from the description, recognize Pestilence among them.

A great deal, of course, could be written about the occurrence of animals and animal imagery in both eastern and western religion between biblical times and today. One feature which I have always found charming and delightful is the accretion, in folk culture, of legends, stories and songs connecting birds and animals with Christian lore and traditions. These have, of course, sprung as a natural phenomenon from what Jung calls the collective unconscious. St Eustace, for example, was a popular saint in medieval England (a thirteenth century sculpture of him can be seen at Wells cathedral). Legend tells that he was originally a Roman general, named Placidas, under the emperor Trajan. One day, while hunting, he encountered a magical stag bearing between its horns the figure of Our Lord on the cross. He gave up his fortune, changed his name and devoted his life to Christ's service. The incident of the stag has also been attributed to St Hubert, and is plainly one of those medieval legends, like William Tell or the dog Gelert, which have become attributed to different heroes and different places. (One must remember that to medieval people stags were a more common sight than they are today.)

The rise, in the sixteenth and seventeenth centuries, of the Protestant ethic and of Puritan idealism had, if anything, a suppressant and distorting

St Eustace, by Pisanello – fifteenth century. (Reproduced by courtesy of the Trustees, The National Gallery, London)

effect on animal imagery in religion just as – or so I think most people would now agree – they had upon a normal and balanced approach to sexuality. (As late as the nineteenth century, to many Protestant clergy all dancing was *ipso facto* wicked; and Thomas Hardy never forgot his father telling him of the callous and barbarous burial, in unconsecrated ground, of a seventeen-year-old girl who had killed herself after bearing an illegitimate baby.) In his book *Man and the Natural World* (Penguin, 1984), Keith Thomas, History Tutor at St John's College, Oxford, stresses that in this country, during the sixteenth to eighteenth centuries, orthodox religious thought emphasized the clear distinction to be drawn between humankind and all other species. 'He that hath well learned. . .wherein a man doth differ from a brute, hath laid such a foundation for a holy life, as all the reason in the world is never able to overthrow.' (Richard Baxter, 1615-1691). 'If a man's mind is not pure,' said Oliver Cromwell, 'there is no difference between him and a beast.' The fact that we ourselves are animals and possess animal nature as an integral part of the human psyche would have been unacceptable to

The Lady and the Unicorn – fifteenth century tapestry. (Musée Cluny)

Cromwell. Yet no English general has left behind him so unenviable a reputation for pitiless ferocity. *Naturam expellas furca, tamen usque recurret.*

I cannot resist quoting, without comment, one of my favourite passages from Tolstoy's *War and Peace*. The date is 1812. Pierre Bezukhov, a Russian aristocrat, has become a prisoner of the French and is forced to take part in the terrible retreat from Moscow. Making a friend of a fellow-prisoner, a peasant named Platón Karátaev, he finds him full of humility, kindliness, homely wisdom and an uncomplaining acceptance of suffering.

> Platón shifted his seat on the straw. After a short silence he rose.
> 'Well, I think you must be sleepy,' said he, and began rapidly crossing himself and repeating 'Lord Jesus Christ, holy Saint Nicholas, Frola and Lavra! Lord Jesus Christ, holy Saint Nicholas, Frola and Lavra! Lord Jesus Christ, have mercy on us and save us!' he concluded, then bowed to the ground, got up, sighed and sat down again on his heap of straw. 'That is the way. Lay me down like a stone, O God, and raise me up like a loaf,' he muttered as he lay down, pulling his coat over him.
> 'What prayer was that you were saying?' asked Pierre. 'Eh?' murmured Platón, who had almost fallen asleep. 'What was I saying? I was praying. Do you not pray?'
> 'Yes, I do,' said Pierre. 'But what was that you said – "Frola and Lavra"?'
> 'Well, of course,' replied Platón quickly. 'The horses' saints. One must pity the animals too.' And again turning over, he fell asleep immediately.

(Tolstoy's Note: Florus and Laurus, brothers who were martyred under Diocletian, are saints of the Russo-Greek church and are reckoned the patron saints of horses by the Russian peasants, who mispronounce their names.)

The subject of animal symbolism in the human psyche, and in humanity's attempts to feel after and express the divine, is virtually inexhaustible. I would like, in conclusion, to quote two passages from C. G. Jung's autobiographical *Memories, Dreams and Reflections* (Collins, 1983). In the first, Jung is speaking of his feelings, when a young student in Switzerland in the late nineteenth century, about the place of animals in the society of his day.

> The more I read and the more familiar I became with city life, the stronger grew my impression that what I was now getting to know as reality belonged to an order of things different from the view of the world I had grown up with in the country, among rivers and woods, among men and animals in a small village bathed in sunlight, with the winds and clouds moving over it, and encompassed by dark night in which uncertain things happened. It was no mere locality on the map, but 'God's world', so ordered by Him and filled with secret meaning. But apparently men did not know this, and even the animals had somehow lost the senses to perceive it. That was evident, for example, in the sorrowful, lost look of the cows and in the resigned eyes of horses, in the devotion of dogs, who clung so desperately to human beings, and even in the self-assured step of the cats who had chosen house and barn as their residence and hunting-ground. People were

like the animals, and seemed as unconscious as they. They looked down upon the ground or up into the trees in order to see what could be put to use and for what purpose; like animals they herded, paired and fought, but did not see that they dwelt in a unified cosmos, in God's world, in an eternity where everything is already born and everything has already died.

Because they are so closely akin to us and share our unknowingness, I loved all warm blooded animals, who have souls like ourselves and with whom, so I thought, we have an instinctive understanding. We experience joy and sorrow, love and hate, hunger and thirst, fear and trust in common – all the essential features of existence with the exception of speech, sharpened consciousness, and science. And although I admired science in the conventional way, I also saw it giving rise to alienation and aberration from 'God's Word', as leading to a degeneration which animals are not capable of. Animals were dear and faithful, unchanging and trustworthy. People I now distrusted more than ever.

In the second passage Jung is recounting his reactions to animal experimentation, while studying anatomy as part of his medical training.

After my first introductory course I became a junior assistant in anatomy, and the following semester, the demonstrator placed me in charge of the course in histology – to my intense satisfaction, naturally. I interested myself primarily in evolutionary theory and comparative anatomy, and I also became acquainted with neo-vitalistic doctrines. What fascinated me most of all was the morphological point of view in the broadest sense. With physiology it was just the opposite. I found the subject thoroughly repellent because of vivisection, which was practised merely for purposes of demonstration. I could never free myself from the feeling that warm-blooded creatures were akin to us and not just cerebral automata. Consequently I cut demonstration classes whenever I could. I realized that one had to experiment on animals, but the demonstration of such experiments nevertheless seemed to me horrible, barbarous and above all unnecessary. I had imagination enough to picture the demonstrated procedures from a mere description of them. My compassion for animals did not derive from the Buddhistic trimmings of Schopenhauer's philosophy, but rested on the deeper foundation of a primitive attitude of mind – on an unconscious identity with animals. At the time, of course, I was wholly ignora of this important psychological fact. My repugnance for physiology wa‚ so great that my examination results in this subject were correspondingly poor. Nevertheless, I scraped through.

'A primitive attitude of mind – an unconscious identity with animals' – this is what we all have in common, whether we like it or not. I have endeavoured briefly to illustrate how deeply human beings have always identified, in thought and imagination, with the countless other creatures with whom we share existence. This is not to argue that there was ever a time when animals were not exploited by man, or when they were treated with true compassion. That is not my point. My point is that man, universally, has never been without a deep consciousness of the animals as a vital part of the divine order, and accordingly has felt towards them what can only be described as wonder and reverence; and this, even where an animal was hunted and sacrificed.

What conclusions follow from this truth must remain a matter for individual determination, in the light of reflection upon the question of what man's relationship should be, today, to other creatures. My own view coincides with that expressed in a treatise entitled 'Dives and Pauper', which was written – as we are told by Keith Thomas in *Man and the Natural World* (Penguin, 1984) – not later than the year 1410. The treatise argues *inter alia* that the commandment against murder, while it does not forbid the slaughter of animals 'when it is profitable for meat or for clothing', or necessary 'to avoid nuisance of the beasts which be noxious to man', does prohibit killing animals for cruelty's sake or out of vanity. And God, it goes on, will take vengeance on those who misuse His creatures. 'And therefore men should have ruth (pity) of beasts and birds and not harm them without

Trapped and trampled to death for the fur on its back. (Lynx)

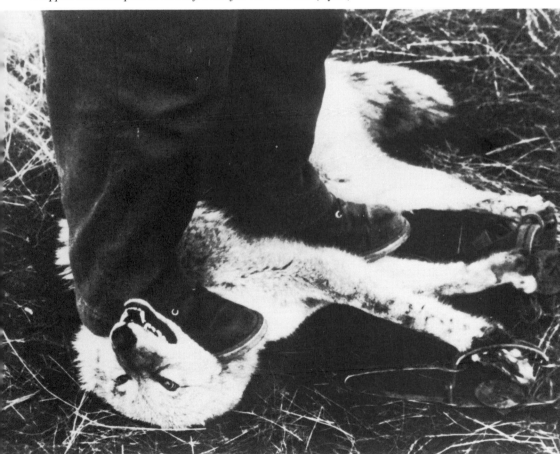

The beauty and dignity of the wild. (Hugo van Lawick)

cause. And therefore, they that for cruelty and vanity torment beasts or fowl more than is speedful to man's living, they sin full grievously.'

For me these words by a medieval Christian writer, obviously felt to constitute a valid application of Our Lord's teaching, hit the nail precisely on the head as regards the luxury fur industry, circuses and zoos. None of these can possibly be argued to be necessary to our living. All 'torment beasts and fowl' for 'vanity' – that is, for nothing more than adornment, so-called entertainment and amusement. The animals not only suffer for no justifiable reason; what is obscene is that they are robbed of their *dignity* and natural animality. This is why circuses and zoos are, literally, blasphemous in the light of the history of animals in religious imagery.

As I have endeavoured to show, religious imagery, when it involves birds and animals, inescapably invests them with or emphasizes their dignity. That is precisely why, in fact, they are brought into the picture – to exemplify and illustrate the beauty and dignity of creation. I wish it were possible to argue that because animals form part of the human religious imagination, it follows that human ethics have required them not to be ill-treated. That, of course, is not the case. As we all know, they have often been ill-treated on that very account, e.g. for sacrifice; in the pursuit of cults and so on. But what I believe one *can* argue is that, because it is indisputable that animal imagery is inseparable from all forms of religion, primitive and modern, people should be continually conscious of the wonderful and spiritual quality of animals,

Robbed of the dignity of the wild. (Mail Newspapers)

and not think of them as if they were no different from boots or electric light bulbs. An animal which is garlanded with flowers and sacrificed is not, perhaps, robbed of its dignity. Animals in traps, circuses and the old-fashioned type of zoos are. A friend of mine, an eminent Harley Street doctor, told me recently that he could not forget having seen, in Chester zoo, a bear, confined in a cage too small and empty to provide it with any comfort, continuously walking along one side, up, back and down. Every time it reached a particular spot, it sat down on its haunches and rotated its rump three times. At this the children – and the adults – laughed.

Let us do all we can to restore to the animals, in our minds, the dignity of which the fur trade, zoos and circuses rob them. That dignity, as I have tried to show, is inseparable from our own, for it lies within our very souls and is expressed in our religious imagery. If we rob the animals of their dignity for nothing but our so-called amusement, we are, by that act, lowering ourselves too.

Roland Boyes

Lobbying for Parliament

Roland Boyes, MP for Houghton and Washington and previously Member of the European Parliament for Durham (1979 to 1984), has for many years taken an interest in the welfare of animals. He is a patron of Zoo Check, and since becoming an MP in June 1983 he has taken up this issue in Parliament. He started his working life as a schoolteacher in Durham and prior to becoming an MEP he was an Assistant Director of Social Services for Durham County Council. He is married with two grown-up sons.

I suppose my first move in this arena occurred many years ago. A beautiful dog, heavy with pregnancy, was apparently about to be shot with a twelve-bore shotgun. Her life was pleaded for and my parents agreed that my sister and I could keep her as a pet. We had many years of enjoyable company from the dog.

My life in those long-gone boyhood days was far from angelic. But I never joined the ranks of those who found 'adventure' in animal suffering. I had an instinctive abhorrence against cruelty to animals. Bird-nesting, fishing, hunting, were pursuits best left to others. Two particular incidents confirmed that all was not well in man's attitude to his fellow creatures.

One involved a visit to Belle Vue Zoo in Manchester. The sight of a majestic elephant in chains, so obviously restricted in his movements, dampened my initial ardour for that outing. The other had brought me to a circus. This was an even greater shock in terms of the ill-treatment of the animals in the name of entertainment. It was all so unnatural. Even as a child, it seemed so evident that the behaviour of the animals was the result of fear and cruelty. Subsequent antagonism towards the very concept of circuses (degrading both for the animals and for the humans who watch the spectacle) dictated that my own children would never want to visit such exhibitions, or even to watch them on television.

Opposition to zoos and circuses, and to cruelty towards animals in general did not, of course, lead me directly into the ranks of 'official' animal welfare sympathizers. It was to be many years later, as a Member of the European Parliament, that events stimulated an interest in this area of political work. Certain issues were attracting some focus in the debating chambers and committee rooms of Strasbourg. There was a growing awareness of the appalling sufferings imposed upon our fellow creatures in European factory farming. Contacts with the Inter-Parliamentary Group on Animal Welfare led to information on various scales of horror. Geese, for example, grossly overfed in order that evening dinners and social gatherings in Paris and elsewhere might feature yet another delicacy for the human participants.

There was also an increasing recognition of the major crisis facing a whole range of endangered species. The net result of this overall attention was that the EEC was forced to consider some tentative, reluctant steps against both the miseries of factory farming, and for the protection of endangered species.

Moving from Strasbourg to Westminster, a change of emphasis was immediately detectable. At the House of Commons the major thrust of lobbying for animal welfare seemed to come from anti-vivisection groups. The catalogue of crimes inflicted on animals in this area is a long and

No room to spread their wings. (Compassion in World Farming)

particularly sorry one. The experimental laboratory is often the ultimate torture chamber for the monkeys, dogs, rabbits, and many other species who have the misfortune to find themselves as the focus of man's 'research'. Recent legislation has received a fair amount of publicity. In essence, it has been a failure in terms of achieving any improvement of the situation behind the doors of this sector of British science. Dissection, poisoning, and deaths of animals will continue in the name of research for cosmetics, tobacco and alcohol. So will the LD50 test. (The LD50 stands for the 'lethal dose' which kills fifty per cent of the animals it is administered to.) The Draize test on rabbits will be unhindered – which effectively means that noxious substances will continue to be dripped into the eyes of rabbits.

Other horrific practices have been endorsed by the new Animals (Scientific Procedures) Bill, including perhaps the most indefensible of them all, the testing of chemical agents on creatures in preparation for using such chemical agents against our own species. Some might claim that a degree of experimentation on animals is necessary on the grounds of health research. Leaving aside the ethical complexities of this argument, it is still debatable whether a vivisection-based curative health service is actually the best route towards the provision of better medical care for adults and children. But the idea of infecting and poisoning animals in order to find more efficient ways of infecting and poisoning ourselves is particularly difficult to justify. Overall, the Bill has not helped the plight of the laboratory animals. A new administration is needed in order to start afresh in legislation

The LD50 test. (Animal Aid)

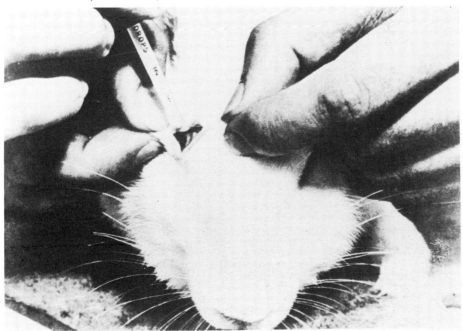

in this field. It was for these reasons that I joined a small minority of MPs who voted against the 1986 changes.

Animal experimentation may have been high on the recent agenda. This is not to say that it has obscured my own preoccupation with that other area of cruelty to animals which had concerned me all those years ago in that visit to Belle Vue in Manchester. Zoos remain a cause of fundamental suffering. Some conditions may have improved since the chaining of that elephant at Belle Vue, but the basic roots of cruelty cannot be eradicated.

Elephants, for example, are part of a roaming, social herd. Their natural habitat involves travel over great distances in search of food and contact. Confinement in an alien environment cannot but lead to cruelty and suffering. This unnatural aspect of animal imprisonment applies to the overwhelming number of species to be found in zoos. Protection from enemies, and the removal of the quest for food, inevitably release the animals from their natural activity in the wild. Strong, deep instincts are frustrated. Chronic anxiety, boredom, and various manifestations of psychological disturbance can and do result from this confinement. The problem of the polar bear, for example, can generally be seen by even the

Great oceanic creatures limited to small pools.
(S. R. Whyte)

most impervious of zoo visitors and spectators. Imprisoned in its limited domain, the polar bear paces to and fro, reflecting a condition of behaviour known as 'stereotypy', severe mental disturbance. Its breeding rate is poor, cub deaths are over twice as high as in the wild, and the alien nature of the habitat has led to mutilation of off-spring and of mates. Other species share similar kinds of suffering, from the great oceanic creatures limited to small pools, to the imprisoned reptiles throwing themselves at the artificial glass barriers in their aquarium tanks.

There have, of course, been attempts to improve the conditions in zoos through government legislation. The new Zoo Licensing Act made some attempt to improve the situation for imprisoned animals in Britain. Certainly, attention to the caging conditions, with focus on the natural behaviour of the species can lead to some progress in this sphere. But the, long-term goal of abolition of zoos must never be relegated to a low priority. The right to imprison animals has to be constantly attacked and questioned by campaigners. There must be no drift towards the building of 'better' zoos at the expense of real conservation projects and ideas.

The often-repeated justifications for zoos have never really stood up to detailed analysis. Education for the public, for example, is a weak argument for these institutions. Species are clearly in an unnatural habitat. In the age of the film and wildlife documentary, there can be little value in keeping animals in captivity in this context. Furthermore, the absence of realistic information on the issues facing wildlife and the environment means that awareness on these matters is not to be stimulated in zoos. Other claims, to the effect that zoos research against disease and seek to pursue real conservation policies, are usually without adequate foundation. Even breeding in captivity, which may be useful as a last resort, has its problems, with many animal behaviour patterns being genetically inherited. This again ensures the familiar suffering which their fellow creatures from the wild already face.

There may of course be a case, in the short term, for specialized centres – establishments where genuine scientific conservation can take place, alongside real education of the public on environmental issues. Such centres should focus on biological study and, in particular, concentrate on efforts to assist endangered species. Breeding of such species may well be justified. On occasions, there is always the possibility that such 'zoos' can be the last refuge for wildlife. The panda, for example, has notorious breeding problems, due to inherent difficulties in fertility and sexual cycles. Perhaps in that situation, its last hope lies in temporary captivity.

In my own area, the Washington Wildfowl Park is playing a key role in assisting the endangered species of the various birds which have been brought to the Centre. Some wild fowl are held captive in the sense that the flight feathers on one wing have been removed to comply with the Wildlife and Countryside Act (1981). The long term aim with the European species is to have them all free flying and breeding and maintaining numbers in the wild.

Free-flying, captive-bred Barnacle Geese. (The Wildfowl Trust)

Alternatives to zoos have to be found and supported. Projects such as that recently undertaken in the Tsavo National Park show us the way. There, a new scheme involving the endangered black rhino has been started. Special fencing has been erected in order to protect the creature from would-be hunters and captors. The ultimate aim is the removal of the artificial protective barriers – a return to the wild itself. Such sanctuaries can provide good protection for endangered species without the stress and deprivation associated with the alien environment of the zoo. They can also help to preserve many other species of animal and plant life in such areas. Examples abound of difficult, but attainable, processes of re-introduction into the wild. Work done by George Adamson in the Kora Hills with lions shows that rehabilitation is possible. Similar successes have been achieved with leopards and other species.

At the end of the day, finance has to be concentrated on supporting the wildlife where it belongs – in the wild. Genuine conservation projects have to take precedence over any backing for 'improved' zoos. National parks are vital factors in protecting the world's species from the intrusion of man.

National parks, and the protection of the natural habitat, may well provide a major part of the answer to the crisis facing wildlife and endangered species. At present though, national parks stand in isolation from the surrounding environment. Less than two per cent of the earth's land is available as a reserve for wildlife – much of the world's areas, rich in animal and plant life, are not under protection at all. This is inevitable, given man's attitude to the environment and the world's resources. Conservation and preservation is not the name of the game. Far from it. The path currently pursued is one of destruction.

Our interference in the processes of evolution and nature is unparalleled. The very balance of nature is being undermined. Species of plant and animal life are facing threats of catastrophic proportion. There is a danger of an eventual breakdown of the ecosystems. We are fast approaching the stage when, unless we conserve our natural resources, and work for greater environmental protection, our children may well inherit a planet which is virtually uninhabitable.

The World Conservation Strategy (WCS), among others, has confirmed this menacing situation. It spoke of the threat against the life support system of the biosphere (the thin surface layer of the earth which maintains life).

The message was a stark one. The WCS had pointed out the human capacity for both creation and destruction. It called for a maintenance of genetic diversity in animal and plant species, as well as general assistance for the ecological processes and life support systems. It also reiterated that use had to be made of the earth's species and ecosystems. In this context, basic truths have to be re-asserted. Quite aside from ethical and aesthetic arguments for conservation in this sphere, people have to recognize the other values of wild animal and plant life. They supply many of the basic ingredients in human life – they are sources, directly or indirectly, of food, shelter, firewood, clothing, medicine and income. Losses of wild strains of crops, for example, have a potentially disastrous impact on world food production.

We can, quite rightly, argue for a different route on the aesthetical and ethical base. We can, more so, focus on the need for ecological diversity and stability, and upon the importance of genetic resources. This is the area which carries real weight with most people. The appeal must go out to man's instinct for his own survival. Conservation of species should be seen for its benefits in terms of agriculture, technology, and general resources. We are so busy destroying species and their habitat that we have not stopped to consider the actual and potential benefits from their existence.

And so it goes on; a planet facing pollution of its air, water and soil. Acidification, acid rain, is rife. This discharge of sulphur dioxide into the atmosphere due to the combustion of fossil fuels, particularly in electricity generation and motor vehicles, affects the lakes and rivers. The result is profound damage to the aquatic life in them and to the water supplies for all forms of life. It has its impact upon the forests and the soil itself. Discharge of nuclear and chemical waste proliferates. The race to pollute and consume quickens by the minute.

The hand at work, of course, in all of this is that of man. It is clear, for example, that the major cause for the colossal loss of the earth's animal and plant life is the endless penetration of the natural habitat pursued for

Beech dieback in the New Forest, England. (Friends of the Earth)

economic exploitation. The drive for rapid consumption of the world's resources is unprecedented. The dangers related to soil erosion mean that many recent food output forecasts could be undermined. Cropland is also badly eroded in this process. Deforestation and over-fishing are features common in areas of the world's richest natural resources.

Much of this activity in the developing world is, of course, inevitable given the gross imbalance between rich and poor. Soil and resources are destroyed out of sheer desperation. Those who advocate conservation of wildlife and of the environment cannot overlook the relationship between the depletion of resources and the needs of millions trapped in appalling poverty and misery. In this context, citizens living in the developed world cannot support conservation of species and natural habitat without supporting better trade-and-aid relations with the developing world. In short, they have to favour a different structure in world economic patterns. Real social and political change is clearly necessary. In addition, the diversion of resources into arms races and the anomalies of food over-production in certain 'rich' parts of the world have to be questioned.

And that is not all. Destruction of resources is far from being a means of meeting the needs of an over-populated world. Indeed, claims that such developments are due to the over-population are just not justified. The fact is that the population is increasing fastest in those countries which are imposing the least demand on resources. The major consumption of global resources lies with the developed world, and in particular among the affluent sector within it. One quarter of the developed world obtains, for example, three quarters of the world's minerals. The multinationals have a vast ability to exploit the world's resources for great profits. By the end of the century, it is estimated that 90 per cent of the global population will have only 20 per cent of the planet's resources. Alternatives to this concentration of consumption must be advocated by all who care about conservation.

There has to be a new awareness in decisions on economic development. Development should occur alongside conservation. The obvious point that short-term exploitation can operate against long-term use has to be re-stated. Greater production has to avoid damaging the natural resources upon which continued production ultimately depends. Environmental recreation and conservation policies have to operate alongside social and economic development. Uncertain risks to the environment have to be avoided. The demand for technical advance has to take into account the indirect and long-term consequences for natural habitats and resources.

Specific and more wide-ranging policies on conservation and environmental

A planet facing pollution of its air. (R. G. Williamson – The Daily Telegraph Colour Library)

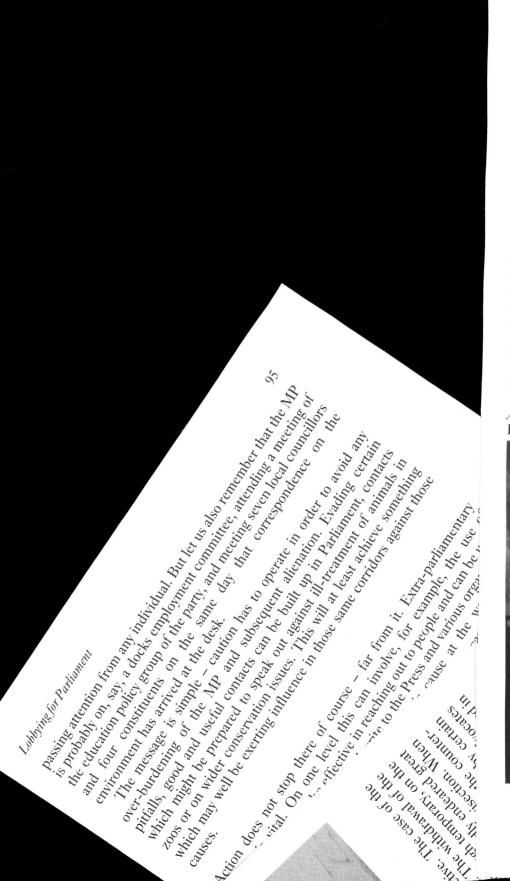

Lobbying for Parliament

passing attention from any individual. But let us also remember that the MP is probably on, say, a docks employment committee, attending a meeting of the education policy group of the party, and meeting seven local councillors and four constituents on the same day that correspondence on the environment has arrived at the desk.

The message is simple – caution has to operate in order to avoid any over-burdening of the MP and subsequent alienation. Evading certain pitfalls, good and useful contacts can be built up in Parliament, contacts which might be prepared to speak out against ill-treatment of animals in zoos or on wider conservation issues. This will at least achieve something which may well be exerting influence in those same corridors against those causes.

Action does not stop there of course – far from it. Extra-parliamentary protection have to be encouraged. On one level, we can seek to encourage changes in individualistic lifestyles and advocate a more ecological approach in people's behaviour. This is all very well, but it remains ineffective unless accompanied by real efforts to influence the corridors of power. It is necessary to lobby the administrative agencies and committees in order to obtain reforms in the numerous areas of the environmental crisis. The policy-makers themselves have to be pressurized and convinced. In the British context, there has to be a combination of parliamentary lobbying alongside direct and active campaigns initiated outside Westminster. In the case of the latter, such lobbying can cross the artificial borders of nations and take on a true international dimension.

Thus, at one level, Westminster has to be tackled. At the outset, it is important to recognize the limitations of Parliament. Powerful external economic and political forces can operate against it. In the age of the EEC, the multinationals, the International Monetary Fund (IMF), and the huge military blocs, its powers are indeed limited. Nevertheless, political parties and MPs do have some influence. They can and do initiate some degree of change through legislation. MPs make use of Early Day Motions (EDMs), oral and written parliamentary questions, letters to ministers, and Private Members' Bills, in order to pressurize, probe, and alter the course of governmental policies both at home and on the world stage. Given this, it is important that there are people at Westminster who are aware of the issues, and who are willing to support initiatives on animal welfare and environmental conservation.

This brings an organization to the complex 'game' of lobbying a seeking to influence in these seemingly distant corridors of power. Pe some obvious ground-rules are worth repeating. Lobbyists have to the level of sympathy for their particular cause. They ca letter-writing or personal contact, or by a combination of can open up a host of previously closed doors, or en brick wall. The approach is so obviously imp remember that the MP's morning mail m document on the economic situation constituents' notes on recent brawls a for the attention of the parliament letters, or indeed leaflets, sho viewpoint, brief, regular impact than a long, d for actual support

Once cont get-togeth name b

Peaceful campaigns. (International Fund for Animal Welfare)

violence is not only wrong, but totally counter-produ 'Mars Bars' poisoning immediately springs to mind confectionery may have had a damaging impact, a manufacturers. But the inconvenience to the numbers of people to the just cause of those action is inevitable. Campaigns again reaction is inevitable. Even the release of ani wings of animal liberation circles must of vivisection. Even the release of ani its capacity for achieving any wor The real route lies in raising a parliaments and outside them needing the world's urgent their habitats, man has conservation. Our con others. We are all P recognize that fact planet, with all its is still time in attitudes. An of campaig

Mark Glover

Can the Earth Survive Man?

Mark Glover's academic background has been in the pure and environmental sciences, having chosen at an early age not to study animals if it involved their having to be killed to do so. He has shown a lifelong interest in natural history which, since the mid-seventies, has been compounded by a growing fear of the consequences of the way man is treating the earth and all its creatures. Whilst researching for a doctorate he was offered the job of wildlife campaigner at Greenpeace. During his four-and-a-half years at Greenpeace, Mark worked on the whale, seal and captive cetacean campaigns as well as the fur issue which showed in no uncertain terms the political and commercial reality behind animal exploitation. At the end of 1985 Mark formed Lynx – an organization devoted to combating the evil and cruelty in the fur trade.

Suppose for a moment that we, as a species, could start again. Imagine being able to wipe the slate clean to restructure our society completely in all its aspects. Included in this would, of course, be our relationship to our surroundings of industrial and agricultural bases and the consequent impact on the environment.

Would we, after such a process, reach the same position that now faces us in the latter years of the twentieth century? Would we, for instance, set about wiping out the species which have already disappeared from the face of the earth? Would we denude the land surface of quite so much of its rain forest, would we plan to use our irreplaceable mineral reserves at quite such a rate, would we pollute our fragile environment to such an extent, and would we rely on a system of weapons of apocalyptic force to 'keep the peace'? One shudders at the notion. Yet there are many today who think that we, humankind, are 'doing all right'. Governments and captains of industry alike are optimistic and portray a rosy picture of our present state of affairs and our future prospects. But, with re-election or next month's sales figures on their respective minds, they would, wouldn't they?

Those who put forward a more gloomy picture are, by and large, dismissed as 'doom-mongers' and it is exceedingly tempting to accept this rejection and to put out of one's mind the reality of the prospects which now face us. As the situation worsens, however, the 'doom-mongers' voices are being taken more notice of.

The first views of earth from outer space visually brought home to people the fragile quality of our own planet. Like a bright blue/green gem suspended in an infinite black abyss the pictures we saw and the experiences of the astronauts took on a near mystical quality. Yet the conditions suitable for us to live in exist only on the surface of this tiny speck in space. Like the shell of an egg, our biosphere, the life supporting system on which we wholly depend, is a thin layer coating the planet.

The fragile quality of our planet. (ESA/Meteosat – The Daily Telegraph Colour Library)

The earth is approximately 4,600 million years old and the miraculous combination of elements and energy from which all life originated occurred some 3,600 million years ago. This extraordinary beginning led to a long slow period of evolution and development during which time the atmosphere in its present form, as well as the other frameworks for life, emerged. Over a period of billions of years a lump of dull, barren rock was transformed to an oasis of life and variety.

It was only relatively recently, within the last few hundred million years, that the species that we are familiar with began to appear. David Attenborough in *Life on Earth* (Collins, 1979) puts this enormous timespan into perspective by comparing the 3,600 million years of biological development to a more tangible calendar year. Thus, life began on the stroke of twelve at the start of the New Year. It was not until September that the first ferns, higher plants and fish evolved; the reptiles did not appear until late November.

The dinosaurs dominated the planet for approximately 160 million years – about two weeks on our contracted calendar – during which time, on 9 December, the first mammals evolved. Not until 7.00 pm on 31 December, the last day of the year, did the first man-like creatures walk the earth and *Homo sapiens* arrived just in time to welcome in the New Year at 11.15 pm. It was not until 11.58 pm that man began to cultivate the soil and a mere two seconds to midnight before the Industrial Revolution took place. With a third of a second to go before the chimes marked the end of the year, the first atom bomb was detonated.

So the period that we have held dominion over our fellow creatures and been able to exert complete influence over our surroundings has been minute when compared with the history of their development – yet our actions have been formidable, shocking and unpardonable.

Man's list of 'crimes' against nature and the natural world is enormous and frightening. Estimates of just how many species we have already wiped out, together with those that are due to be eliminated by the year 2000, vary, as does the area of tropical rainforest that will have disappeared, how much carbon dioxide will have been pumped into the atmosphere to enhance the 'greenhouse effect', or what proportion of our mineral reserves will remain for future generations.

Catherine Caufield's *In the Rainforest* (Heinemann, 1985) vividly portrays the stark reality of deforestation. Before man had any interest in tropical rainforests they covered five billion acres of the world's surface. Today, half of these lush rich areas have been destroyed by man, mostly during the last 200 years, and there is no sign of a let-up in this relentless devastation. Recent studies have put the current rates of deforestation at between 14 and 50 million acres each year. That is about 30 acres every single minute. The Food and Agriculture Organization of the United Nations predicts that 20 per cent of all remaining rainforest will have disappeared or be severely degraded by the end of the century. Consisting, as they do, of such a wealth and variety of plant and animal species, this dramatic loss of rainforest inevitably results in extinction of species – some of which disappear never having been recorded by man. Others are exterminated directly by simple over-exploitation.

Currently between 500,000 and one million species are threatened with extinction, that is one in ten of all species thought to exist and, if current trends continue, as many as a quarter of all species may have vanished by the middle of the next century.

And yet, what is our response to this critical state of emergency? Millions and millions of people every year visit zoos around the world believing them to be oases for these endangered species, where they breed very successfully until one day when miraculously they will be returned to the wild. All of the literature and propaganda from the zoo world reinforces this view, and the money paid over by the visitors is done with the thought that at least some of it is going to the cause of conservation. Every year zoos around the world spend many times over the combined incomes of all conservation organizations, but their contribution to the saving of endangered species is negligible by comparison. Worse than the monetary aspects of this imbalance is the psychological effect that zoos have. People really believe that captive, caged groups of animals are a solution to the decimation of the world's natural areas which continues unabated.

At the same time we are using what is left of our precious mineral reserves at alarming rates. According to *The World Index of Strategic Minerals* by Hargreaves and Fromson (Gower, 1983) at current levels of consumption the known deposits of many important metals will be exhausted within one generation. Silver, for instance, will be mined out in 25 years, cadmium in 40 years, copper in 65 years, tin in 40 years and all known deposits of gold will have been extracted in 30 years time. Now many lengthy arguments take place over how much of these elements can and will be recycled, or what new deposits may be discovered, but one thing is clear; we will, quite soon, have used up all of the natural deposits. They are finite; that is a fact.

The World Index calculates that, at current levels of exploitation, natural lead reserves will be exhausted in 45 years. Lead is of immense importance for use in batteries, alloys, plumbing and the chemical industry, and yet each year we squander more than a quarter of a million tonnes of this precious metal by its most infamous and useless usage – its unnecessary addition to petrol. This quantity is then pumped into the environment from car exhausts. This simple process thereby converts a valuable finite resource into a deadly poison which threatens the lives and development of our children.

Oil itself is running out and, at current rates of consumption, all known reserves will be drastically depleted within 35 years.* Again, new discoveries and a more conservative attitude as the price of oil rises may prolong its availability, but the end of oil is in sight.

---

* *Gaia Atlas of Planet Management* (Pan, 1985).

The burning of oil (and other fossil fuels) results in another form of insidious but very real air pollution. Carbon dioxide is only a minor constituent of our atmosphere. In fact it constitutes 0.0345 per cent of the air we breathe (345 parts per million) but it plays a vital role in the temperature balance of the earth via the 'greenhouse effect', whereby radiation emitted by the earth is absorbed and reflected back by the carbon dioxide molecules. Any increase in the amount of carbon dioxide in the atmosphere increases the amount of reflected radiation, causing a consequent rise in the average temperature at the earth's surface. Even small changes in the carbon dioxide concentration can have measurable effects on our temperature through this subtle mechanism. Since 1850 the carbon dioxide level has increased by nearly 30 per cent – virtually all of which can be attributed to the burning of fossil fuels by man.

A major study carried out for the United States Department of Energy has recently reported that by the end of the next century temperatures may well increase to levels not reached for at least 100,000 years due to this effect, with consequent repercussions on sea level, agriculture and other human activities so profound that we ought to be planning for them now.

From physics we learn that entropy, a measure of a thermodynamic system's degree of disorder, can only increase or remain constant, so that our universe is tending towards the complete disorder of its particles. Our use of the world's precious mineral deposits appears to follow the essence of this physical law in a remarkable and reckless fashion.

The catalogue of man's abuse and over-exploitation of the planet and all of its parts is extensive and well documented in many places. We live in a world fast running out of many of the materials which form an everyday part of our lives. Our seas and land masses are already contaminated with pollutants as

River and sea pollution. (Greenpeace)

well as with radioactive waste that will remain hazardous for tens of thousands of years. Many of the unique creatures that we share the planet with face complete annihilation at our hand.

We know all of this, we can argue over figures and how long certain materials will last or certain processes take, but one thing is sure – there can be no doubt that we are, through our actions, transforming, bit by bit, the paradise that our species emerged from into a wasteland, and as a species we face many hardships, much suffering and even our own demise.

How can this situation have arisen? The short term approach and relationship with the environment, on the face of it, makes no sense, so how could it have come about?

The history of commercial whaling is a vivid example of how this predicament has been reached. Species after species of the world's great whales have been systematically over-hunted since whaling began.

At first, the slower swimming right whales were all that could be caught when the motive power of the hunters was provided by wind and sail. With the advent of steam-powered ships in the mid-nineteenth century, however, all whale species became targets for the hunters. Today the minke whale, the smallest of the great whales, is the mainstay of the industry. All of its larger cousins have been hunted to the point where it is no longer commercially viable to pursue them. In the Antarctic, former stronghold of the blue whale, the most colossal animal ever to have graced our planet, there may be as few as one thousand individuals left where, before whaling, hundreds of thousands roamed in peace. The species may yet die out altogether in the area due to its extreme scarcity.

Why is this, when the International Whaling Commission (IWC) – whaling's governing body – purports to support and abide by the notion of sustainable yields? An understanding of the answer to this question gives an insight into the short-term thinking and decisions that governments and large industrial concerns alike adopt.

Economics and the competitiveness of industry direct that it is in a company's interests to exploit a resource as quickly as possible and then use the profits from that operation to finance its next investment. Thus the whaling companies themselves have no interest in any whale harvest in one or two hundred years time, more in the level of profits for the forthcoming and immediately forseeable whaling seasons. These depend on taking the maximum number of whales. In fact, the IWC was originally established by whaling countries in an attempt to stabilize the supply of whale products onto the market place rather than to protect whales.

Similarly, what real interest could the governments that constitute the IWC's membership have in the long-term fate of the whales? Their primary concern is short-term – that of maintaining domestic popularity, or of keeping up with their international competitors in the space, arms, industrial growth or whatever, races. Often, then, the interests of governments and industry coincide and the exploiters work hand in glove with the state. The

Flensing of a fin whale, Icelandic coastal station. (Greenpeace)

two have evolved in a symbiotic fashion to ravage and denude the planet.

As the stock of the earth's resources declines, competition will inevitably increase for what remains. Those not already in the forefront of the race will be left further behind, and the dream of more equal distribution of wealth will remain a dream. Current international negotiations regarding exploitation of the ocean beds or of Antarctica, even though no minerals are proven to exist in the latter, bear this out totally. The other consequence of there being less cake to share out is that a more unscrupulous attitude will characterize ever more desperate efforts to obtain these resources. Safeguards to the environment, while exploitation is underway, will be exaggerated, the potential impact of actions glossed over, and the harm and despondency that we shall all face if these developments do not occur will be constantly referred to – all so that the last few drops of oil or tonnes of metal can be extracted with little or no protest.

Throughout history each extreme abuse, iniquity or immorality has produced a reaction from a faction within the community of ordinary people. Tyranny, oppression, hardship, starvation and cruelty have always been met by a level of opposition. These movements have invariably been made up of a wide spectrum of views and have usually included extreme elements, prepared to go to extraordinary lengths in attempts to further their own causes. Whether it is a suffragette who throws herself under a king's horse, students occupying buildings, anti-war protestors setting themselves on fire or an animal rights demonstrator breaking into a laboratory, almost every form of protest can be linked with more extreme actions.

Somewhat akin to Newton's third law of motion, most protests prompt if not an equal then certainly an opposite reaction. Protest and lobby groups that actively campaign take on many forms and can be both for or against a particular cause. Some, like multi-national companies or the National Farmers Union (NFU) are very well funded and use political lobbying professionally, either to bolster their position or to counter any attack on their activities made by opposing protest groups. These organizations can be characterized as having broadly similar goals as governments, and are for the most part self-interest groups. Those who challenge the views of these groups, or their practices, often find that they are taking on not one, but two, major strands of opposition – one, unscrupulous and directed by self-interest, the other whose main interests are short-term and overshadowed by the spectre of re-election. Often the distinctions are blurred, and governments commonly act without honour in such matters and may resort to underhand tactics or even, in the case of the sinking of the Greenpeace boat the *Rainbow Warrior*, terrorism.

Examples of such behaviour are manifest, from oil companies deliberately misinforming the British government over the issue of lead in petrol in order to delay the implementation of legislation, to the mid-nineteenth century mill owners who claimed that widespread bankruptcy would follow the introduction of the Factory Acts. The Canadian government made similar, unsubstantiated claims when faced with protests against the clubbing to death of a quarter of a million harp seal pups each year. The argument it advanced was that if the commercial motive was removed from the hunt then the exercise would have to continue, at the same level, in order to protect the dwindling stocks of fish. As soon as the European Community, the main source of demand for the skins of baby seals, banned their import, the hunt ended. But the truth, that over-fishing by man was the real cause of the disappearance of the fish, has conveniently been brushed aside. So the oil companies, the mill owners, even the Canadian government have been involved in obvious and blatant attempts to hoodwink both the public and even other governments. Experience has shown time and time again that people, institutions and governments with vested interests can never be trusted on such matters. Here, a clear distinction can be drawn between pressure groups such as the NFU or the Law Society – the self-interest groups – and those formed from a sense of moral duty or even anger at what is seen to be wrong and in need of address. Often these more altruistic organizations find themselves at odds with large vested interests or the intransigence of the status quo. Relying on public goodwill and generosity for their funding, they often find themselves entering such uneven contests severely handicapped.

For a fair assessment of potentially damaging initiatives or of the claims made by this or that pressure group it ought, in theory, to be possible to

The death of a seal pup.
(International Fund for Animal Welfare)

design an even-handed, impartial enquiry system where both sides are provided with, or limited to, the same resources to enable their case to be made. The public enquiry system in this country, where David and Goliath contests rage over nuclear power stations or new motorways, has obviously failed, and falls far short of an ideal system. Perhaps no such system exists, but at least something like the environmental impact assessments undertaken in the USA give a limited platform for putting over all sides of an argument before any decisions are made.

Although the RSPCA dates back to 1824, animal welfare and environmentalism, as subjects of concern, have come about mostly since the turn of the century, with the more radical and challenging philosophies arising in only the last few decades as the full horror and extent of what we were doing to our planet and fellow creatures emerged. Many of these new

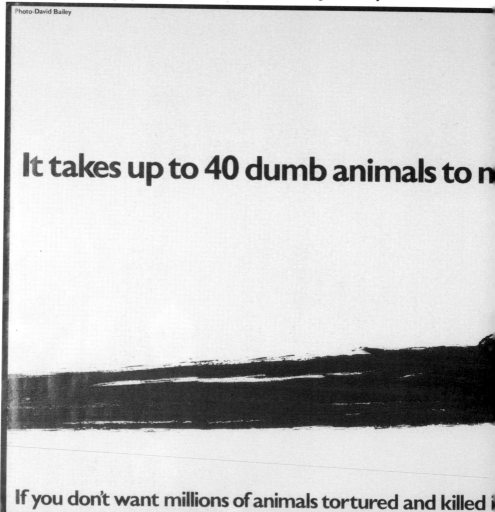

Photo: David Bailey

It takes up to 40 dumb animals to m

If you don't want millions of animals tortured and killed

organizations and ideas seek to influence our own behaviour, sometimes calling for a fundamental re-thinking of our individual or our collective relationship with the environment and its inhabitants. This is, after all, what is sought by most campaigning groups – meaningful and lasting change which is reflected in public opinion.

There are almost as many groups campaigning on behalf of the environment or animals as there are tactics adopted to achieve their desired goals. Many of the established and well-known groups involved in these areas are barred from overt political lobbying by their charitable status and the archaic rules that govern charities in the United Kingdom. Lobbying has been used very successfully by many of the self-interest groups as well as other pressure groups such as consumer bodies and penal reformers. There has emerged a whole profession and infrastructure around this stratagem,

a fur coat.

But only one to wear it.

LYNX

Fighting the fur trade
PO Box 509 Dunmow, Essex. Tel: 0371 2016

old traps, don't buy a fur coat.

and clearly defined ways of using political lobbying can now be identified. With very few exceptions the new, more radical, environmental and animal groups have failed, so far, to have had much impact in this area of campaigning. This may well be due to a combination of lack of experience in the art of political lobbying, a distrust of parliament and a frustration with the time it takes to introduce change, combined with a simple lack of funds. However, it must be recognized that this form of campaigning can be very effective and it must not be dismissed by the animal rights and environmental movements, for it is a legitimate and effective tactic. But only as a tactic, since, unlike many of the reforms sought by groups such as the consumer organization which can be brought about by new legislation, what animal and environmental bodies seek is more fundamental.

Whatever cause a pressure group wishes to introduce to the legislative process it has to be able to put forward a case based on rational argument which would include questions of morality, social responsibility and so on, as well as to be able to demonstrate that it has wide public support.

Here we come to the crux of the matter, since public support is the key to fundamental change. Widespread public involvement provides a way of tackling what appears to be the fairly insoluble problem of governments and other vested interests working together for their own ends and carving up what is left of the earth whilst severely mistreating our fellow creatures along the way.

The usual history of a campaign by a pressure goup is that a problem is first identified and then researched to ensure that the original beliefs and inferences were correct, so that a strategy and a set of tactics can then be developed and undertaken. These can involve lobbying governments, the EEC, international conventions, local governments etc. Petitions, the production of research and lobbying material, letter writing campaigns, demonstrations and direct action can – and are – all used to good effect. Some organizations are prepared to break national laws set by governments, maintaining that higher moral or natural laws exist and that, in fact, it is often the governments themselves that violate these laws to the long term detriment and cost to the planet, animals or to ourselves.

In recent years, non-violent direct action has played an increasingly important and successful part in the work of many pressure groups. It is used as a dramatic tactic designed to highlight abuses that would not normally receive publicity. Indeed the perpetrators of these abuses often try to avoid the public eye. Examples include the placing of small inflatable boats between whaling vessels and their fleeing prey, or protestors chaining themselves to anything appropriate or hanging off high buildings with banners. The images stick clearly in our minds which is, after all, the purpose of the event. Such actions are designed to create a platform for the particular cause – be it whaling, or the banning of nuclear weapons, or acid rain. Not having the same resources as those they protest against, groups find resorting to these kinds of tactics a very effective means of getting their case across to a wider audience.

The reaction of the public to what they discover and learn from these actions is what can be used to bring about change. It is the stimulation of that reaction which is all important. Pressure groups, unlike governments, are very small, and so their powers and influence are usually very limited. All too often the pressure group is seen and treated as a thorn in the side, or a nuisance, by the government or company that is the target of its attentions. The actual role that groups play in the modern world is more like that of terriers snapping at the heels of a monolithic and destructive giant. Victories are being won but the machinery of devastation is still clanking along relentlessly.

When a pressure group embarks upon a particular campaign it starts off having nothing to lose. The situation is usually dire, so the group can only improve things. It is therefore the function of a pressure group to press for beneficial change. Usually it has no bargaining counters on its side and so the offer of 'negotiation' is of little benefit. This does not rule out discussions, or even gradual reform, but it does mean that the pressure group has to create the climate of conditions to enable change to take place, or actually to bring about the change itself.

It is the pressure created by the public that effects change of a lasting nature. Governments come and go but people are the constant factor. Laws can be and have been revoked. They are made by governments whose responsibilities are essentially limited to a small number of years and which usually have re-election hanging over their heads.

We, all of us, come on to this planet inheriting an environment, infrastructure and body of learning, information, philosophy and experience which we have a clear moral duty to leave to the next and subsequent generations. An almost paradoxical situation has arisen in that the duties and responsibilities of governments do not, in the long term, coincide with our own, as a species.

With the benefits of experience and knowledge of the planet, we are capable of, and should be, improving conditions on earth, and actually be repairing some of the damage instead of letting the decline continue.

The only way for this to happen is for ordinary people to become more involved with the issues of modern pressure groups. It is all too easy in the world today to leave decision and policy-making to politicians and experts. Indeed this passing of the buck is encouraged, and its proponents use their own language and jargon to confuse and to ensure that this is the case. Of course we cannot be experts on all matters, nor do we have to be, but it is the duty of individuals to take more interest in their surroundings and the direction in which they are being led. People basically know when something is wrong or right, and this is borne out by the growth of the various pressure groups and the strength of campaigns to save whales or stop nuclear power. 'Experts' do not always speak from an unbiased perspective. Who these experts represent and their motivations, be they prime ministers or zoo owners, should be held in question constantly and their statements never

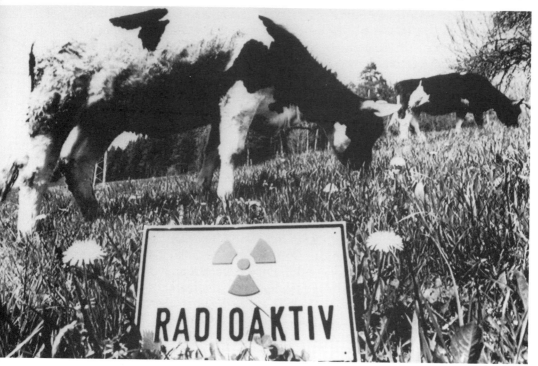

International fall-out. (Chernobyl disaster). (The Associated Press)

accepted at face value.

A prime example of how people can influence events once an abuse is brought to their attention took place in 1978. The previous autumn the British government, responding to an ill-founded case put forward by Scottish fishermen, attempted to introduce a 'management plan' designed to halve the population of grey seals in the UK. Bad weather saved the seals in that year but twelve months later the hired Norwegian killers, once more tried to begin slaughtering seal pups, despite the protestations of the conservation groups. Seeing no alternative, Greenpeace took its ship, the *Rainbow Warrior*, to the Orkneys and let it be known that its members would place themselves between the hunters and the seals if any attempt was made to kill the animals. The press interest was extremely high and the public became quickly aware of the plight of the seals on their bleak breeding beaches. The response, measured in tens of thousands of letters to the Prime Minister of the day, James Callaghan, proved decisive, and the management programme was abandoned, pending the results of a scientific examination of the situation. This research eventually demonstrated that no level of reduction of the population of grey seals would measurably increase the amounts of fish available to the fishermen, and the idea of killing seals was officially finally, abandoned.

Within days of the explosion at Chernobyl, world leaders and the nuclear industry, almost with one voice, stated that 'a similar accident could not happen here' and that the 'nuclear power programmes must continue'. How easily and quickly they dismissed the incredible scale of the disaster that occurred; the fact that between 25,000 and 48,000 people will, it is estimated, die prematurely from cancer as a result. Equally easily glossed over and ignored is how the peoples of affected countries now have genuine fears for their own future and for that of their children.

Individuals – all individuals – must voice their fears and concerns. Great changes are ahead: materials are beginning to run out, more species are becoming threatened by extinction, and our seas, rivers, land, even the air that we breathe is becoming more and more polluted. We are rapidly approaching the point where the short term 'sticking plaster' solution to our problems will no longer work.

The power that individuals have is vast and it is the behaviour of individuals that most pressure groups seek to influence. Do not buy fur; do not visit zoos or circuses with animals; use cosmetics that have not been tested on animals; feed the starving; begin to adopt an energy system that relies upon renewable resources, and so on. Sadly the list is long and it is a measure of how precarious and obscenely immoral our present position is, but simple choices and logical changes in behaviour can overcome them all. People have to gain more confidence in their ability to influence events, their elected leaders and the future.

One recent experience has dramatically and sadly shown governments in their true light, and how much notice they take of the wishes of their people in these matters. Bob Geldof's magnificent efforts to relieve starvation in Africa captured the imagination of people around the world, culminating in the 'Sport Aid' events which were billed as the largest petition in the world, and timed to perfection to have maximum influence on world leaders attending a UN conference on the Third World in New York. Despite the scale of participation and level of commitment from millions of people who were prepared to add their voices to a call for change, their leaders let them down extremely badly. The wishes of individuals were not translated into action and a unique chance to affect real and lasting change was missed.

The work of pressure groups continues, and indeed such organizations provide the best way for people to become more involved in crucial issues; but on its own, membership of such groups is not enough. It is a change in outlook and behaviour which is so vital. The understanding that governments will not, and pressure groups cannot, save the planet, or cause us to adopt an animal right's philosophy or a balanced environmental programme, is essential. Only a concerted change in outlook and behaviour will bring about lasting, meaningful change.

Over and over again governments, or the apologists with vested interests in ruining our planet, have been proven wrong in what they say. Governments have, until now, paid only the slightest attention to what pressure groups stand for, and only then when forced to at the last minute. This is due to their panic over the need to be voted in for another term or to

Chimpanzees (Hugo Van Lawick)

Baron Hugo van Lawick

Individuals in the Landscape

I nternationally famous wildlife cameraman and winner of an Academy Award for the wildlife series 'Jane Goodall's World of Animal Behaviour', Hugo van Lawick was born in Soerabaje, Indonesia, and educated in England and the Netherlands. In 1959 he joined Armand and Michaela Denis in East Africa as a wildlife cameraman for their TV series 'On Safari', then as a cameraman and still photographer in East Africa for the National Geographic Society. From 1967 he has lived most of the time in a tented camp on the Serengeti in Tanzania, where he has made a series of award-winning films and authored (and co-authored) a number of best-selling books.

I do not believe in any life hereafter and this probably explains my belief that the quality of life for every individual creature on earth is almost sacred. However, death can be preferable to a life in captivity. For instance, I remember a scientist, studying psychology, showing me a monkey which he had reared in almost total isolation. Each time the scientist flicked his fingers in threat at the monkey, the poor creature, unable to get at its protagonist, redirected its frustration by biting its own arm. Not only was this a pathetic sight but, to make matters worse, the scientist was amused by this behaviour. It demonstrated a lack of moral feelings and showed that he was not a profound thinker. A pity, since basically it was mainly his brain which made him different from the monkey. Even his brain is not as superior as has originally been assumed, because it is now known that apes, such as chimpanzees, have a far greater brain power than was previously imagined. This should not be too surprising because if one believes in evolution then the abilities and behaviour of man did not suddenly emerge from nowhere, but developed from something which was already there.

If one accepts that the apes, and specifically chimpanzees, are our closest living relatives, then it should be possible to determine to some extent the behaviour and abilities of prehistoric man. This is because it is reasonable to suppose that any similar behaviour patterns, found in both men and chimpanzees, were probably inherited from their common ancestor.

The most obvious behaviour patterns which occur in both chimpanzees and man are the various submissive, reassurance and greeting gestures such as bowing, embracing, kissing, and even handkissing and handshaking. Undoubtedly, these gestures were used also by prehistoric man. I remember being taught as a teenager at school that handshaking evolved from showing you had no weapon in your hand. In fact, it is a combination of a submissive gesture (holding out a hand) and reassurance gestures (holding and patting). Gentle physical touch is reassuring not only in man and the apes but also among other creatures. For instance, when an elephant is slightly nervous another may reassure it by touching it gently with its trunk.

The need for reassurance starts to give some idea of the emotional feelings of other creatures. If one accepts that other creatures have the same or very similar emotional feelings as humans, then it becomes easier to imagine the suffering they are subjected to when kept in captivity and used in experiments. Of course, in addition to mental suffering, extreme physical suffering is also often involved during experiments on animals.

Man's attitude to animals was undoubtedly first formed during evolution, when prehistoric man and certain animals competed for food or preyed upon each other. Man started to get the upper hand when he invented primitive weapons, and it may be no coincidence that the disappearance of many of the larger creatures in prehistoric times corresponds to the appearance of the first stone tools. This may seem strange because it is generally believed that man started as a scavenger before becoming a hunter. However, studies of animal behaviour do not support this assumption. First of all, scavenging is almost impossible except for creatures such as vultures which, in flight, can cover hundreds of square miles daily in search of food. Animals such as jackals and hyaenas, generally believed to be scavengers, in fact mainly survive on prey caught and killed by themselves. A further clue that prehistoric man was a hunter before he also became a scavenger is provided by chimpanzees, our closest living relatives, who hunt but do not scavenge.

One would expect that prehistoric man would have avoided the large animals and concentrated on the smaller ones. However, when watching the various sized predators on the open plains of East Africa today, it is striking that the smaller animals are often at an advantage because they are quicker. Thus I have seen a lone hyena tackle a rhino calf even though the mother rhino was standing next to it. The adult rhino was just not quick enough to

The difference between freedom and captivity for a vulture. (main picture – Hugo van Lawick/inset Virginia McKenna)

be able to defend its calf. In addition, predators living in groups are often at an advantage. For instance hyenas chase off lions from a kill on many occasions. Prehistoric man, organized in small groups with weapons and with his higher intelligence, should have been well able to tackle large animals. Undoubtedly, over a period of time, man began to feel superior and this feeling was substantially accentuated by many religions which, in the extreme, encouraged him to believe that animals were created for him to do with as he liked. These religions, in effect, elevated man to a sort of god over other creatures, with a right to decide which will live and which will die and which will suffer first before dying.

When, during more recent history, man wandered further afield than his immediate surroundings and saw things new to him, he became an extensive collector, keen to show strange objects, including dead animals and later live ones, to his companions or fellow men in his own area. Today, this should not be necessary. We have films which can show far more clearly what animals look like and how they behave. Collections in zoos are therefore an outdated concept. But those involved with zoos, like any special interest group, desperately think up all sorts of excuses why they should exist and, I must add, often believe their excuses to be valid. The main reason we are given is their important role in the preservation of species. Yet most animal species kept in zoos are not, at this stage, faced with extinction. In fact, the species saved from extinction by zoos can probably be counted on the fingers of one hand, or two hands at most. More importantly, if the money spent on zoos by governments and individuals was made available for conservation, most of the species kept in zoos would be safe in the wild. I heard of $10 million being spent on gorillas in captivity. One can imagine how well the

Hyenas tracking a rhino calf with its mother. (Hugo van Lawick)

gorillas in Rwanda (and a few other places) would be protected in the wild if anything like that sort of money was available.

A further excuse is that, in captivity, the natural behaviour of the animals can be studied. However, this will rarely give accurate information; it is like a visitor from another planet trying to discover normal human behaviour by watching the inhabitants of a mental institution. Certainly chimpanzees in captivity behave abnormally and, if they were humans, would be considered to be in need of psychiatric treatment. Secondly, I suspect that some scientists working in zoos want the best of both worlds: to study animals and to be able to enjoy comforts of a city and a home. The last thing they want is to live in the wild. Others, who would like to work in the wild, are unable to obtain the necessary funds. In fact, much of the money spent on zoos would be better used funding valuable scientific research in the field.

Another excuse for the existence of zoos is that they create an interest in animals, especially among children. This is true but, undoubtedly, the interest by children would be fostered equally by 'zoos' containing the large variety of domestic animals which exist, and by showing interesting films on wildlife. There is little doubt that the falling attendance at zoos is due to the effect of wildlife films, and the greater awareness this has created among the public of the artificiality of zoos and the immorality of keeping wild animals in captivity.

The general public is also becoming more aware of the fact that capturing wild animals for marketing to zoos, to private individuals and to laboratories, causes intense misery. How different these attitudes are to ten or twenty years ago when the general public was not aware of the truth, and wildlife trappers were usually considered heroes, often made popular in Hollywood films.

It is now widely known that young chimpanzees are caught by shooting their

mothers. Since many of the youngsters are also killed during this method of capture, or die subsequently due to bad treatment or disease, it is estimated that between five to ten chimpanzees die for every one that reaches a zoo or laboratory. Those which die are undoubtedly better off. In West Africa, for example, I saw a young chimpanzee for sale in a basket-shaped cage made from dry palm fronds, and so small that the creature could not move. It had originally managed to get one hand out of the cage. To prevent this the chimp's captor had tied its fingers tightly to its wrists with some wire. It had remained like this for two months before being confiscated. When we took the chimpanzee out of the cage and untied its fingers, they were stuck back and never recovered. Nor could it move at all for some weeks. Today, many years later, it is able to move but its fingers are still deformed and the only way in which it can climb a tree is by using its wrists.

Some young chimpanzees are bought by photographers who entice tourists to be photographed with the creatures. Such chimpanzees often have a short life. They are expensive to feed and so are often killed at the end of the tourist season and new ones bought at the beginning of the next. This behaviour was extensively reported as occurring in Spain. Atrocities, such as I have described, will continue as long as people visit zoos, allow themselves to be photographed with captive wild animals and so on. They only occur because there is a market for captive animals, and anyone supporting that market is supporting such atrocities.

In Africa I regularly see wild birds, such as colourful lovebirds, caught during the breeding season, being transported in cages both inside vehicles and on roof racks. I have seen these vehicles driven through extreme heat, tropical downpours and cold nights in a race to cover a distance of 200 miles

Lovebirds. (Hugo van Lawick)

or more. It is amazing that any of the captive birds can survive at all. The death rate must be extremely high, especially when one includes the abandoned youngsters which have starved in their nests. Anyone wearing anything made from wild animals or keeping them captive is helping to exterminate those species in the wild. Obviously, if there was no market, the legal and illegal trapping and killing of animals would come to an almost complete halt.

When talking about conservation it is usual to discuss the preservation of one or more species. Individuals are generally considered of little importance. I believe this attitude to be wrong. Individuals are important, even among plants! For instance, two grains of rice may well have saved millions of people from starvation. In the 1960s a virus was affecting rice production. There was no known protection from this major disease and so the International Rice Research Institute investigated about 10,000 varieties of rice, hoping to find a resistant gene. Finally, they looked at a hundred seeds of a single variety which they had in their collection and found that two of these seeds had a resistant gene. So they went back into the wild to collect more specimens. However, none with the resistant gene was found ever again. Now every modern rice plant has a gene which originated from those two vital wild seeds. This, and the fact that about 7,000 medical compounds have so far been extracted from plants, should have been an extremely important lesson to man of the urgency of preserving the large variety of plants. Yet man daily exterminates plant species at an accelerating pace.

The day will come when an epidemic of a new disease sweeps among mankind, but the plant which could have cured it has been exterminated. This may well be a disease which could kill 25 per cent or more of the human population of the world. The Black Death is an example of what can happen. Unfortunately, it is generally believed that modern medical science can develop cures without the aid of plants. This is a dangerous and mistaken assumption. For instance, malaria parasites are adept at becoming resistant to all known quinine substitutes. Recently, a deadly strain of malaria evolved in East Africa and spread, endangering the lives of millions who live in or visit the tropics. Luckily, although the strain was resistant to quinine substitutes, the malaria parasites had not become resistant to natural quinine. Accordingly, neglected plantations producing quinine have now come back into production.

Many plants cannot survive without animals. They help during the reproductive cycle of the plant by, for instance, transporting the pollen from one plant to another, Furthermore, medical compounds derived from plants often consist of naturally produced poisons which deter animals from eating the plants. Remove the animals and, over a period of time, the plants are likely to stop producing the useful compounds.

Usually, farmers consider many species of animal as pests, especially insects, and therefore resort to insecticides. However, these often kill the predatory species which help the farmer. It has been found in many cases that, by using insecticides, the farmer is in fact worse off. Frequently, not only do some pest insects survive but multiply much faster than normal once their natural predators have been more or less exterminated. This occurred when DDT was used on lemon trees to destroy red scale insects, and when pesticides were used on oil palms which were suffering from outbreaks of bagworms and nettle grubs. In both cases, some time after insecticides were used, the pest species increased many times over their original numbers.

An interesting event occurred with oil palms, native to Africa, which were cultivated in large plantations in Malaysia. It was found that the trees had to be pollinated at great cost by human hand. The Unilever company went to enormous trouble to discover which wild creature in Africa pollinates oil palm trees. It turned out to be a weevil and, subsequently, much costly research was conducted to determine whether this weevil would be harmful if released in Malaysia. The conclusion was no, and so now African weevils, imported into Malaysia, pollinate the oil palms.

The increase of a prey species due to the decrease of its predators is not only relevant to insects. I remember as a teenager visiting a forest in Belgium and being surprised at the large number of rodents. The local gamekeeper explained that he shot all birds of prey, the natural predators of the rodents, 'because they kill song birds and the local pigeon keepers' association pays a reward for each pair of talons.' However, it is dangerous to assume that killing a predator will automatically result in an increase of its prey. Predators tend to kill the less healthy individuals and, by doing so, decrease the danger of disease spreading through the prey population. In Africa, fish often abound where crocodiles, their main predators, are numerous. Thus, for instance, fishermen wishing to cull seals may well be misguided: culling seals may result in less fish. The size of animal populations is determined mainly by the amount of food available and may only be slightly affected by the number of their predators, apart from man. The decrease of fish yields in the seas, lakes and rivers is almost always as a result of man's activities. However, on occasions, any decrease may be an illusion! For example, if a salmon fisherman in Alaska had started his profession in 1910, he might well have complained bitterly by 1950 that the number of salmon had decreased drastically. In fact the total yields of salmon remained roughly the same throughout those years, but instead of about 1,000 boats fishing for salmon in Alaska, as was the case in 1910, there were approximately 10,000 boats by 1950. So by 1950 our hypothetical fisherman was catching only about a tenth of the number of salmon he caught in 1910.

Misguided attitudes about predators were, and still are, common in Europe with regard to foxes, and in Africa and Asia concerning jackals. They are often accused of killing farm animals, including lambs. Unfortunately, whenever a fox or jackal is seen eating a lamb, it is generally assumed to have killed it. A misguided assumption, I would suggest. Though their usual food is rodents, snakes and insects, which they kill for themselves, undoubtedly jackals and foxes do occasionally kill lambs. However, I feel that the help

Jackals. (Hugo van Lawick)

that jackals and foxes afford the farmers, as effective forms of pest control, far outweighs the harm they do in taking the odd lamb.

Furthermore, since, to my knowledge, no one has yet done any work to determine the proportion of lambs actually killed compared with the proportion scavenged, it seems extreme and blatantly unscientific to conclude, as one scientist in southern Africa did, that if the stomach of a jackal contains remnants of sheep then the predator had killed the sheep. I believe, therefore, that in most cases farmers would find jackals and foxes to be useful species.

Foxes always bring to my mind fox hunting in England. I listened in utter amazement to a representative of this 'sport' claim, not only that it was not cruel, but that the fox enjoys it! An utterly inane remark, obviously made by someone who has no understanding or knowledge of animal behaviour. I have seen predators pursue their prey on thousands of occasions and have never seen any indication that the prey animal enjoyed it.

To call killing for fun a sport makes a mockery of the word 'sport'. Hunters often argue that hunting is an instinct. In fact, the concept of instinct is over used and applies equally well to, say, picking your nose. Most people manage to resist that temptation and most people live quite happily without killing. In fact, when hunters use instinct as an excuse, they are implying that they have more primitive instincts and so are less civilized than those of us who do not hunt. So why do some people like hunting as a 'sport'? The reasons, as far as I can determine, differ between individuals and include those who genuinely like nature but feel they should actively be doing something while in the wild, those who are trying to prove they are brave, those who are trying 'to keep up with the Jones's' and those trying to make money.

I think the first and second category would find more satisfaction in watching animals and trying to photograph them. If they want danger they

The end of a day's sport. (League Against Cruel Sports)

could decide to use a standard lens only, so that they would have to get very close to potentially dangerous creatures. The third category would automatically follow suit and the fourth might try to make money by producing wildlife films. Whatever the reasons for each individual who hunts as a 'sport', it often means that they do not understand or fully appreciate animals and, frequently, indicates an immaturity of mind. It is interesting in this respect that many hunters in Africa as they become older (and wiser) stop hunting, and are often embarrassed about their past hunting days.

A good knowledge of animal behaviour is likely to stop anyone wanting to kill animals. Many years ago I made a film on wild dogs, concentrating on the individual personalities of each dog in one pack. Prior to this film wild dogs had generally been considered vermin by hunters, and often whole packs were shot on sight. During this period of making the film I was in frequent contact with a hunter, who was a friend of mine, and through my stories and subsequently on viewing the film, he got to know the wild dogs as individuals. To my delight he finally confided, with no prompting: 'I will never again be able to shoot a wild dog. I know them too well!'

When looking at human emotions, the degree of involvement an individual

Cape hunting dogs. (Hugo van Lawick)

will feel in response to a disaster will depend on how well he or she knows the victims, i.e. whether a family member is involved (worst case), a friend is involved (not as bad as a family member) and finally whether the victim is unknown (the least bad of the three). However, the emotional response in the latter case is increased if the personality of the victim is known – for instance when a film star dies. The same is true of animals. A dog owner may be very upset by the death of his own pet but less so when a dog, belonging to a friend, dies and much less so when the dog is unknown to him. If he has never had a cat he may not care at all when a cat dies.

These degrees of emotional involvement can be used when making natural history films. I know that I can involve the general public to some degree by teaching them about wildlife in this way, but I also know that I can increase this involvement considerably if the film concentrates on individual animals. The stronger the personality of the animal, the greater will be the emotional involvement of the viewer. Subsequently, having got to know a member of a species as an individual with its own personality, it becomes easier to imagine other members of that same species as interesting individuals as well. The viewer is then more likely to be emotionally involved when one of that species is mistreated or killed.

Most people do not have the opportunity to get to know animals in the wild and are therefore dependent on films to obtain their knowledge and understanding. Although some people like watching wildlife films, others do not, and if the aims of conservation are to be realized, and it may be too late, it is vital to try to increase the interest of those who normally do not watch them. This can only be done by making the films more attractive. This means a greater emphasis on story content and drama, and animals as individual characters, and less, I think, on the straightforward educational (documentary) style films. This does not necessarily mean they will be inaccurate. It is perfectly possible to make educational films with strong story content and drama which, at the same time, show true animal behaviour.

In attempting to capture drama in wildlife films great care must be taken, for wildlife film makers may well destroy their trade if they use animals as unfeeling tools. The general public is not stupid, and as the knowledge of photography and animal behaviour increases, they will have a good idea which sequences in wildlife films were staged and which were not, no matter how well the photographer thought he had staged the event at the time. This will undoubtedly result in anger with the wildlife photographers concerned and a rejection of their films. This anger may well be transferred into a mistrust of wildlife films in general. In addition, if wildlife photographers, supposedly conservationists, are prepared to mistreat individual animals, then why should the general public feel differently? How any photographer can be proud of his results when they are due, for instance, to the release of a captive prey animal in front of a predator, is beyond me. Maybe their only aim in life is money and fame. The dramas which occur naturally in the wild are far greater than those which have been staged. To be able to photograph such events requires patience.

In this chapter I have touched on a number of ways in which animals are mistreated. I am not among those who view the future pessimistically. After

Ostriches on the plain. (Hugo van Lawick)

all, 25 years ago few people had heard about conservation. Now, although most people agree with its aims, too few do anything about it, since they have the mistaken view that there is little that they can contribute. This is not true.

First of all, if each individual decides not to visit a zoo, not to buy products made from wild animals, not to keep wild pets and so on, it will make it less worthwhile for trappers and poachers to ply their trade. Furthermore, if a large enough percentage of the population considers it immoral to keep wild animals in captivity, to wear their skins and to hunt for fun, it will be impossible to ignore this groundswell of opinion. Every individual can play a part in this.

I once took an acquaintance out to supper who was wearing a coat made from serval cat skins. She excused herself, saying it had been given to her many years ago. I explained she was helping to encourage a fashion which is based on killing. I also told her the true story of a trapped leopard which was killed by poking a red hot poker up its anus in order not to damage its valuable skin. We are still good friends but she has never worn that coat since. Each of us can help to make such fashion unpopular among our friends and acquaintances. This in turn may snowball to make the behaviour socially unacceptable. The wearing of skins belongs to the prehistoric times of cavemen.

It is often pointed out that wild animal products are an important source of foreign exchange in poor third world countries. Though true, the argument would become invalid if more funds were made available by richer countries for conservation in the third world. The income from hunting in a given area could be exceeded by the revenue from tourism, if that same area were made into a National Park. As the world becomes more populated and the increasing numbers of city dwellers have more leisure time, the urge for vast numbers of them to experience areas of natural beauty and watch wildlife will increase greatly. Already some National Parks can barely cope

with the numbers of people visiting them yearly.

Any country with sufficiently large, varied and well organized National Parks will, undoubtedly, take the lion's share of the future income from tourism. For instance, in Tanzania the authorities have successfully protected their National Parks and Reserves and are still designating new areas. At this stage they should receive considerable financial and moral support to help them succeed in their aims. If their conservation strategy is successful I have no doubt that, though one of the poorest countries in the world today, Tanzania will become one of the richer countries in the future. The big problems which third world countries encounter in trying to protect their wildlife areas are all related to money. On the one hand the governments need financial help to protect their wildlife, while on the other hand certain individuals try to make money by the legal and illegal trapping or killing of animals in order to supply the existing market in richer countries. The trouble is that among the individuals involved in illegal trapping and killing are some who have been appointed to protect wildlife and the environment. These people make it impossible to accomplish the task of conservation for the future. Governments could be helped considerably by the establishment of highly trained international anti-poaching teams, possibly under the auspices of the United Nations. At the request of the relevant government, teams could be rapidly despatched to trouble spots – their unexpected arrival giving the poachers and racketeers no warning.

Politicians determine to a large extent the laws by which we live – laws which will only be enforced by popular support. It is becoming increasingly clear that more and more people want conservation. Any company which is involved in the irresponsible exploitation of natural resources will find in the near future that a large section of the public will boycott its wares. Similarly, any politician who does not actively support conservation is unlikely to be elected. By not buying those wares and by not electing those politicians we can start the process of getting the message across now.

Arjan Singh

Wild Life Conservation – a Modern Concept

A rjan Singh is a distinguished naturalist and one of India's most active conservationists who has devoted his life to the study and protection of the great cats. For over 25 years he has lived at Tiger Haven, a remote farm on the edge of the jungle just over the Nepalese border, and he played a leading role in the setting up of the Dudhwa National Park, a forest sanctuary adjacent to his land. He is author of *Prince of Cats* (Cape, 1982), *Tara a Tigress* (Quartet, 1983) and *Tiger, Tiger* (Cape, 1984). He was awarded the World Wildlife Gold Medal in 1976.

A succession of muted growls erupted into full throated roars as Tara threatened me on the bank of the river Neora. Too late I realized that I had come between her and her two cubs, aged about two months old, hidden away in a ravine. She made a mock charge as I called to her, but branched off behind some bushes from where she continued to snarl. This was my erstwhile hand-reared tigress who had opted for free living eight and a half years ago, yet she shared the Tiger Haven Range with me, and still accorded me recognition. The demonstration was a warning in defence of her cubs.

The great cats are dangerous only in very special circumstances, for Nature does not allow her children to get mixed up in a fracas which might mean injury to the mother and starvation for the cubs. Tara was therefore telling me in no uncertain terms to keep away. Though the wonderful *Born Free* series would never have been published had George Adamson not shot the lioness who charged out in defence of her cubs, I maintain that this was probably a mock charge to warn off the intruder. As if to prove that the demonstration was a special circumstance I called to Tara the next day from a machan near a kill. She was moving away, but as I called her, she stopped and listened. She turned around to walk slowly past me, and into cover in the opposite direction.

Wildlife conservation has been on the human list of priorities for a considerable time. The world bodies of the International Union for Conservation of Nature and Natural Resources (IUCN) and the World Wildlife Fund (WWF) are devoted to the protection of all animal and plant species and their habitats. They seek to reconcile a co-existence between other lifeforms and the uncontrollable human population surge in third world countries, which now remain as the main repository of wildlife. In addition the Food and Agriculture Organization (FAO), the United Nations Development Programme (UNDP), and the United Nations Environment Programme (UNEP) fund wildlife projects, and even the United Nations, the world body for the political guidance of human relations, and on whom we repose a fading hope for future peace, expresses concern for the environment.

The question which haunts all wildlife conservationists is how long will these countries of soaring populations, and increasing demands, have room for wild animals who need a modicum of space and therefore are, of necessity, in competition with humans? Will developed countries with stable populations, who themselves wilfully abused indigenous wildlife, be able to assist in preserving species of other countries?

We have singularly failed to evolve a fresh line of thinking governing our relationship with other natural creations, and in keeping with modern thought processes. Scientific dogma combined with spurious anthropomorphosis govern our system of dealing with non-human species. The 'sport killers lobby' is powerful enough to influence the thinking of even the specialist wildlife bodies. Penal codes are drawn up for intra-specific human behaviour, but we get pleasure out of taking the life of other creatures. Civilized thought does not extend to the suffering of an animal. Elaborate guidelines exist for the speedy despatch of wounded tigers and leopards. We term this operation as 'putting them out of their misery' – irrespective of the cause of that misery – and they are termed bloodthirsty, ferocious, treacherous and unpredictable, merely because they are sometimes smart enough to turn the tables on their heavily armed assailants.

Much 'macho' discussion goes on about the relative dangers of 'hunting the Big Five' in Africa, yet the affection of Elsa the lioness for her human protectors has become a legend. Virgo the wild African elephant recognized Iain Douglas-Hamilton after two years. My leopardess preferred to bring her cubs up in the wild, yet brought them to her human friend when danger threatened. Tara, the tigress, affords me recognition eight and a half years after she opted for free living. Animals have a sense of dignity, and they react to the way they are treated.

When a man kills a tiger he is a 'hero'. When the tiger kills the man he is a villain. It is on this premise that anthropomorphism operates. Except for intellectual functions, all human instincts and senses are similar to animal

Trophies of the sport hunters. (Will Travers)

attributes. Some are more developed, and certain extra-sensory perceptions are non-existent in *Homo sapiens.* Therefore the stigma against the ascription of human characteristics to what is not human cannot be accepted in its entirety, especially in the invidious form in which it prevails at present, where any feeling of sentiment for animals is conveniently described as anthropomorphosis.

It is essential that we should rationalize wildlife conservation, but while doing so we must realize that, though it is an integral part of the conservation spectrum as a whole, it is essentially different from the inanimate environment in that it is in competition with the human, as far as basic resources are concerned. Trees are necessary for human well-being, and we have discovered that if we over-exploit them the 'predictable' reactions are harmful. If we destroy forests we suffer from flooding and erosional siltation, xerofication and the advance of the deserts, climatic changes and instability. We try to remedy this condition by afforestation, and temper short-term human requirements by long-term planning. In other words we endeavour to make the wisest and best use of natural resources.

But when we apply such a yardstick to wildlife we get stuck with the miserable and meaningless cliché that we must preserve wildlife because it may be of use to man at some stage of our voyage of discovery on this planet. We have found that the armadillo is of use to humans for leprosy research, and therefore its utility as an experimental medium to the medical profession justifies its existence. Yet the badger must be destroyed because it is suspected of transmitting tuberculosis to domestic stock. Primates are used for cruel experimentation because of their affinity to humans, and frogs, despite their utility as devourers of agricultural pests, are inhumanely slaughtered to satisfy a gourmet industry in far-away industrially developed countries. When we exterminate a species we sin against the 'law' of evolution.

The Dark Continent was the land of plenty when the white man ruled. But after Independence many African countries were riven by tribal feuds and dissensions, and their economic status is abysmal. Due to developmental malpractices, drought and desertification are wracking the soul of once fertile lands. As the human population skyrockets at an alarming rate, a massive land hunger threatens wildlife tourism, the largest foreign exchange earner of many countries. The situation is made worse by organized poaching, where meagerly armed wildlife guards are overcome by machine-guns financed by wealthy racketeers. The black rhino, of which J. Hunter shot 1,600 while opening up the white Highlands, is now in serious trouble. The status symbol of rhino horn dagger handles in North Yemen, and the horn's supposed medicinal powers (mainly to reduce fevers) in the

Over $2½ million ivory stockpile. (Simon Trevor)

Far East have made the black rhino a threatened species over much of its former range.

Yet in this age of democracy all we can do is try to alleviate the situation. While wildlife habitats are constricted and migration routes cut off, the human race, unable to control its own numbers, has taken on itself, in its arrogance and rapacity, the control of animal populations by the reprehensible practice of 'culling for their own good'. Thus we witness the strange situation of elephants that in some areas face extinction, being culled by the thousand in Zimbabwe. When animal populations are on the increase they are culled in case they over-exploit their habitat. However, as human activity puts increased pressure on wildlife habitat, it is only by manipulating wildlife management practices that we can preserve the last wild environments.

But the principle of wildlife management is vulnerable to pressure from the 'sport killers lobby', anxious to promote hunting as an integral part of conservation. It is so simple to constrict a deficit habitat – one where animal numbers are low – and convert it into a locally surplus one, thus justifying 'sport culling'. South Africa now supports hunting and East African countries are beginning to do the same. Nepal, already devastated by massive deforestation, is now, under the influence of American sportsmen, permitting limited leopard hunting. Hunters, anxious to 'do their bit in the cause of science' now send ear-tags from leopards shot outside protected or study areas to scientists working in the field.

It is worthwhile at this juncture to examine the ethics and methods of 'sport hunting', for it is perhaps this unworthy pastime which, more than anything else, has given our fellow creatures the ignoble reputation which they are unable to refute. In fiction the wolf is big and bad. In reality he leads an exemplary family life, subsists on seasonal prey, and controls his population by allowing only the dominant male to breed. The tiger and leopard are reputed to be ferocious and unpredictable, when it is only the aggressive attitudes of humans which upset their tolerance and essential tranquillity of temperament: and so it continues for all animals capable of retaliation.

The basic question for civilized man is whether it is correct to take the life of another being for the sake of personal enjoyment. Hunters seek to justify their stance by stating that it is not the kill but the chase that matters. The enjoyment, however, can be presumed to be entirely one-sided when, for example, the fugitive fox is pursued by a pack of hounds and galloping horses, urged on by the yells of red-coated huntsmen.

Evil actions which only apply to humans are used to malign wild nature. The terrorists who prowl the airways and the waterways of so-called civilized existence are said to be acting according to the law of the jungle, which is a base canard. Wild animals kill to eat, procreate in season, and their numbers are controlled by natural laws. The 'hawks' at the United Nations sit glowering at each other while the 'doves' seek peaceful co-existence. In nature, the hawk minds his own business when not hunting, and it is the doves who are always squabbling. Domestic dogs are promiscuous in their breeding habits, whereas their wild counterparts are believed to be monogamous.

The macho image created by the hunting of dangerous 'game' is merely a pointer to the ego and the killer instinct of the human, which gives the satisfaction of having humbled a perfect product of many millions of years of evolution. It is a vandalism which does not give the hunted a chance. The use of a modern weapon, with a muzzle velocity of 2,500 feet per second, and an energy of over 5,000 pounds per square foot, is a ludicrous travesty of 'sportsmanship' in the hands of a person seated high up in the safety of a tree. Yet ever more powerful weapons of offence boost the faltering egos of these nimrods – these great hunters. The true hunter is the one who kills for food, and the human undoubtedly qualified for this title at some time during his evolution. But now when achievement has lifted him to the moon, a paranoiac concept has debased him to the status of a vandal.

I look back with revulsion to the days of my boyhood when I shot lizards and small birds: to my youth when I blazed off both barrels of a shotgun at night into the shining eyes of a herd of deer; with a deep regret as, armed with a modern rifle, I stood over the prostrate body of a beautiful young tigress who had sinned against humanity when, bereft of her natural prey killed off in the name of crop protection, she had eaten a human to provide milk for her starving cubs. My evolution into a civilized being was then near completion.

Unfortunately, literature is full of the glories of the chase, and perhaps it is too much to expect that, in the final analysis, we will accept the ignominy or anti-climax of the kill.

Down the ages the human has looked upon the animal as the provider of entertainment – starting with the so-called pastime of 'sport hunting', now mercifully on the way out, not because of any inherent norm of civilized compassion, but simply because, in many areas, there is nothing left to hunt. Safari parks, circuses and zoos are other organizations which depend on animal exhibitions. Safari parks, as a means of making money, have unfortunately devoted themselves mainly to the exhibition of exotic animals, where concern for animal welfare varies in direct proportion to the profits.

Lion Country Safari, in the Laguna Hills of California, made huge profits to begin with, and ambitious programmes of expansion were started. Seventeen tigers were herded into one enclosure in an absurd attempt to turn them in social predators. Hoses were used by concealed personnel to chase lions into the open for the enjoyment of the 'drive through' vehicles. The delights and dangers of the 'African veldt' and the 'Indian jungle' were stressed. But when the profits fell off, the meat rations were progressively decreased. Ultimately the entire operation was closed as the meat ration dried up with the profits. Such conditions apply in larger or lesser degree to most parks, for wildlife must pay for itself – always.

Circuses are another form of entertainment in which the animals' dignity is trampled upon by making them 'perform' tricks. Continuously on the move, the animals are confined in constricted cages and gazed upon by avid crowds – their freedom restrained, and their rations often restricted. Internationally famous circuses like Barnum and Bailey and the Ringling Brothers do exist in plush circumstances in keeping with their status, but lower down the scale horrendous conditions prevail, animals performing demeaning antics to earn their keep, and animal welfare is *non est*.

Zoos are the only organizations which have attempted to justify their existence in the context of modern thought by defining their motives, which are, of course, chiefly concerned with their human impact. Originally zoos were solely for entertainment, and perhaps a nostalgic reminder to the shooting fraternity of the 'battues' they indulged in during the season. Now, however, with wildlife conservation an integral part of human philosophy, governments must be convinced by more cogent arguments of the utility of zoos, for, unlike circuses and safari parks, they are in many countries mainly sponsored by the 'Establishment'.

The main reasons advanced for the necessity of having zoos is that they serve as breeding grounds for endangered species; that they are essential for the scientific study of certain aspects of behaviour and reproductive dynamics, which cannot be studied in the wild; that they are useful for instilling the general public, who cannot afford to visit wilderness areas, with a regard for, and a familiarity with, the indigenous fauna, and that they serve as places of entertainment for the public.

There is no doubt that in developed and affluent countries zoo maintenance and management has in a few instances attained a degree of efficiency in keeping with the dignity of the animal, and though confinement can never be a substitute for free living it can perhaps correctly be said that where habitats are degraded, zoos of optimum standards – like San Diego in California – may be the only hope for wild species displaced by uncontrolled population increases among humans. Yet the trade in animals has exterminated entire gorilla groups in Rwanda and elsewhere, and the memory of Guy the gorilla who spent most of his 30 years in London Zoo alone, still haunts me.

The educative value of wildlife is in reality a meaningless cliché. Animals must be saved for their own sake and not because the public will, hopefully, decree that it should be so. In any case, zoos in developing countries are places of recreation where the public entertains itself by harassing and teasing the animals, and revolting experimentation, like the mating of different species, is encouraged. They should be abolished.

The only positive functions which zoos can serve is as breeding places for endangered species with a view to their reintroduction into their natural habitat, which presupposes an international organization to co-ordinate and control such an operation. However, nowhere has such a co-operative effort been made, and we behold the unedifying spectacle of a limited interchange between zoos, and the vasectomy and euthanasia of valuable exhibits as the bottom falls out of a limited market.

Guy the gorilla. (W. Suschitzky)

The real enemy of wildlife is the democratic process which accords government to the people, for the people and by the people. Other species have no right to exist except through the magnanimity of the indigenous human, and in an agricultural economy a time must come when hunger will claim all available land. An international desire to save wildlife cannot compete with the fierce nationalism that prevails in the present age. The time to change our outlook is imperative, and from now on the conservationist must be served by science. The last battle to save what remains is a crusade. It is only the emotive urge that can inspire us to pursue and attain what appear, perhaps, to be 'lost causes'.

I have worked on the re-introduction to the wild of solitary predators for a period of eight years. I consider this period the most rewarding of my life, and the year and a half during which I lived with a tigress, a leopardess and a small dog was the highlight. The two rival super-predators established a relationship which prevailed, with only minor altercations, during their association. The biblical adage where the lion would lie with the lamb, came to life when my small dog, Eelie, lived in amity with the two big cats and, on the strength of her having been at Tiger Haven before they arrived, would dispossess them of their legitimate kills. In my company their characters developed, as they used to before the human began to harass them, and for a time in their company I felt I had inherited the nobility of the beast.

During 1971 I was given a four-month-old leopard cub. I called him Prince. This was the first major predator I had reared and I did not know what to expect. I found him affectionate and intelligent. Once he made friends with my dog they became playmates, and it was a mutual recognition which sustained their friendship. Other dogs were legitimate prey species, and even Eelie's son, who looked exactly like his mother, was chased with great determination. At two years of age Prince obeyed the call of the wild and left my company, but a year and a half later as he stood one night near my bed to gaze at his little canine companion of yesteryear, I knew that he recollected his carefree youth.

Soon afterwards, I was given two female leopards as prospective brides for Prince, and though one female was poisoned, the other mated with 'my' male and had two families. Her affection for me was overwhelming, and although she instinctively brought up her cubs in the wild, despite the fact that she herself had been reared by humans, she brought them to Tiger Haven when she was in trouble – once when floods threatened her den, and once when she was chased by a tigress and one of her cubs was carried away. She lived with me for nearly six years, and finally died from unknown causes, a hundred yards from her haven which she could not reach.

I applied for permission to try a re-introduction experiment with a tigress, and though the Prime Minister was agreeable, a cub was not available in India. I went to the Twycross Zoo in England to collect a three-month-old tigress, presented to the Prime Minister of India by Professor Grzimek of Germany, for use in a pilot project of a zoo-born tigress being returned to

Arjan Singh and Tara the tigress. (Lisa van Gruisen)

the wild. There were many objections from local conservationists who said that Tara did not belong to the Indian sub-species and would pollute the blood line. This was, to my mind, an astonishing argument as far as conservation went, as of the eight sub-species, three were virtually extinct, four did not have much hope for existence in the future, and only the Indian sub-species might be a candidate for a long term survival if its habitat could be ensured. As the tiger had originated in Siberia, and the sub-species, which had been driven south due to various pressures, had undergone morphological modification due to environmental conditions, there could really be no valid objection to introducing one sub-species into the vanishing habitat of another, in the belief that they would regain their original form over a period of time.

Meanwhile, the subject of this crucial experiment survived the air journey and was gradually introduced to Eelie and Harriet the leopardess. They both recognized the small tigress as a juvenile, but while the dog played with her the leopardess tried to adopt her, as, coincidentally, she was the same age as two cubs which Harriet had lost to a tigress – who had lost her own cubs to a herd of elephants. Though Tara was nearly as large as the leopardess, Harriet's mother instinct told her that this was a possible replacement for the cubs she had lost. Amazingly, the fact that she had been sorely harassed by a tigress did not prejudice her against the species. As Tara grew up with the other animals, behavioural changes took place, and when the leopardess had her cub, Mameena, the tigress became very nervous of the suckling mother, though by now she was considerably larger. After Mameena was weaned the leopardess would again allow the tigress to chase her, and the way she used to look down after climbing half way up a perpendicular tree, made it evident that she was trying to encourage Tara to climb.

Tara took to associating with a young tiger whom I called Tara's Male, who shared the Tiger Haven Range with his sibling Long Toes. In the middle of January 1978 she became mature, when female cubs normally leave their mother, and left my company with the tiger of her choice. For some time there was considerable doubt as to Tara's whereabouts, but her presence was confirmed four months later when Eelie and then Harriet scent-marked a tree which Tara had used. This had been standard daily procedure on an electric pylon when the three animals had been with me.

For two years she shared the range with Old Crooked Feet, an elderly tiger, but perhaps because of natural selection she did not breed, and it was only when Tara's Male had taken over the range in his own dominant capacity that Tara bred with him at five years of age. They had three cubs, a male and two females, and though first-time mothers are supposed to be flighty the young tigress was fiercely protective. Towards the third sibling, who was obviously a runt and suffering from competition from the other siblings, the mother was highly solicitous, and even the father would abandon the kill to let her feed, though literature claims that a male tiger is a menace to his offspring, who are kept away by the mother.

The male cub also regularly associated with his father until, at the age of three, he was almost the same size. Contrary to old literature which holds that big males will oust from the vicinity their growing offspring, especially sons, they used to meet regularly at kills, and one memorable day I watched both father and son sitting side by side in the river. They still associate and, subject to tiger protocol, when only individuals feed at kills at one time, a viable co-existence operates with a tolerance governed by a familial relationship. Tigers have a means of avoiding accidental encounters by roaring, scraping and scent marking. Of course there is a limit to co-existence, and overcrowded ranges have their own system of culling.

The small cub remained dependent on Tara till the age of two and a half, and did not leave till her second family were about three months old. Thereafter she disappeared. One of the sadnesses of living with a growing family of territorial animals is that once they leave to establish territories of their own, one loses touch with them, and the small tigress, so vulnerable and insecure, might well be in limbo without the protection of her mother.

Tara's second family consisted of two females, and though she was solicitous of their welfare she did not react violently to imagined threats to her offspring, as she had with her original progeny. Their father mixed freely with them, but when he moved away to take up with another tigress of his realm, the son of her first family took over the range. She, however, objected to him coming near her cubs and would snarl and growl at him. Though he was by now much larger than her he would initially move away, according to a sophisticated heirarchical relationship, which seems to prevail among animals with blood ties.

The little family grew up until, at the age of fifteen months, one of them went lame. It was not possible to determine the cause. I suspected porcupine quills, for she had wounds on the inside of her forearm and below the shoulder, and another just above her right forepad which she licked avidly. Water seemed to give her relief and she would sit for hours on end in the shallow stream before the arrival of the monsoon. She lost condition and the use of her front leg.

I appealed to the authorities to have her immobilized and medically examined but to no avail. I watched her lying on the wet sand which gave her relief. She was weak and though she realized she was being watched she did not care. It was such a pretty, yet stricken little face, which lifted to look at her human sympathizers, only to flop back again, and I hoped that her mother's care would help her to recover. The human insensitivity to the suffering of that animal is against all means of civilized compassion, and is to our everlasting shame.

My visits to Tara lessened because of her concern for the cub and she now spent much time exhorting her in some way I was unable to comprehend, though the other tigers spent considerable time in the river. One afternoon I heard mother admonishing her daughter beyond a bend in the river, and I sent my tracker to have a look. He hurried back to say that he was greeted by loud snarls from the tigress. I hastened to the spot where

Tara – a free life. (Arjan Singh)

Tara sat scowling across the river, in front of the bushes where the afflicted cub was hidden. We were in full view, but as I called to her, her expression softened, as she watched and listened. For me the clock turned back as the span of the years seemed to fade, and the past merged with the present. By the end of the monsoon the little family had disintegrated.

Despite continued appeals to the authorities to have the afflicted cub immobilized and medically examined, no action was taken. With the outbreak of the rains, the deep and muddy current was no longer a haven of relief. I lost contact, though I continued my attempts at feeding her. An additional complication now occurred, for the male cub, with a confidence born of his range status, took to guarding his kill during the day. Though Tara and her other daughter shared the kills, the lame cub was apprehensive. One morning my tracker came upon the male cub feeding while the lame one sat watching fifty metres away.

Soon after, she left the area and in desperate straits leapt a five-foot wall into the courtyard of a railway pointsman, and killed three goats tethered inside. Alarmed by human shouts, and the passage of a railway train, she performed the astonishing feat of leaping a seven-and-a-half-foot wall to safety – and starvation. A ravening hunger drove her the next night to visit Park Headquarters, where she mauled a cow and chewed the arm of an old woman who was sleeping outside because of the heat.

The danger was now too close for comfort, for the so-called man-eating spectre haunted the hitherto uncaring authorities. Alarmed by its proximity they took immediate steps to trap the young tigress in a baited cage which she entered willingly enough on 1 October 1985. She was sent to the Lucknow Zoo where four captured tigers had already died. It was five months since I had made the first of my appeals. The zoo vets were of the

Incarcerated in the name of conservation. (Bill Travers)

opinion that osteo-myelitis, caused by a poacher's gunshot wounds, was responsible for the bone injury. Due to the delay in treatment a bone graft was now the only cure. Another tiger had been consigned to incarceration and slow death, in the name of conservation.

Tara's Male was absent from the Tiger Haven for over a year, while Tara reared her second family. I speculated whether natural selection would allow her to mate with her son. I dreaded the possibility that I would be a mute witness to the passing of a great ruler, as these magnificent carnivores succumbed to the inevitable conflict between man and beast. I hoped against hope that once Tara's cubs had left her, and she was foot loose and fancy free once more, he would return. In early winter of 1985 Tara's Male returned to mate with his tigress of two earlier seasons. It is possible that in a range only the dominant male breeds for, as is well known, heirarchical animals destroy the offspring of other males to further the prospects of their own genes.

The human has outgrown all these safeguards and safety valves and is now at odds with Nature.

Amen

The sky is burning
the birds have flown
I had so much bread
why didn't I feed them
when there was time?

The wind has changed
I smell burning feathers
The birds, where are the birds?

The seas are boiling
the gulls can't fish
they stand on the shore
watching the molten horizon

Beyond reach
high up the beach
The dying Phalarope –
our last hope
She lies on her back
an oily black.

Spike Milligan

Kieran Mulvaney

Conservation as a Human Problem

Kieran Mulvaney is a young freelance writer on conservation and natural history subjects. A consultant to the People's Trust for Endangered Species, he is also the author of *The Zoo Ideal*, an exposé of the arguments behind the zoo philosophy. As well as conservation and animal rights, his particular passion is for dolphins and whales, and he has edited a book on the relationship between dolphins and humans. In this chapter, hc argues that conservation through captive breeding is far too expensive and inefficient to be of any use in fighting extinction. Furthermore, he says, environmental degradation affects people as much as animals, and consequently it can only really be halted in the long-term by political action.

Beneath the expanse of tarmac and concrete that is Mauritius airport there lie the skeletons of an extraordinary species of bird. A form of pigeon, it was nonetheless as big as a swan; but, despite its bulk, it had only stumpy little wings which were quite incapable of lifting it off the ground. When the Portuguese landed on the island in the 1500s and saw this curious creature, with its huge bill and scaly feet, they named it after its distinctive call. They christened it the dodo.

The demise of this unfortunate bird is, without doubt, the most famous of all extinctions brought about by the hand of man. Having evolved on an island habitat, with no natural predators, the dodo had neither the inclination nor the ability to defend itself against, or take flight from, any potential danger; consequently, the Portuguese had no difficulty in hunting and killing it in vast numbers. Even when humans left Mauritius, the dodo was not safe: pigs which the men had brought with them multiplied, destroying a great deal of vegetation and trampling underfoot the eggs the birds laid on the forest floor. By 1681, less than a century after it had first been described, the dodo was extinct. The dodo's case is not unique. History books abound with tales of similar extinctions – such as those of the Great Auk, Passenger Pigeon, Quagga, Stephen Island Wren and Falkland Islands Dog – all of which disappeared entirely as a result of man's predations. But although the most famous exterminations all occurred pre-World War II, we, too, have our modern-day dodos: species that have been forced out of existence by the pressures of human civilization. Certainly, we have not managed to hunt any species directly into oblivion lately (although we have come dangerously close with the likes of rhinos, Arabian oryx and whales), but, in the last forty years, modern vices such as pollution and, particularly, habitat destruction, have finished off more life-forms than our ancestors could ever have managed.

The International Union for Conservation of Nature and Natural Resources (IUCN) regularly publishes a series of 'Red Data Books'. They make depressing reading. The books list every species of animal and plant known to be in danger of extinction, and their size is testimony to the rate at which we are threatening to push aside our fellow life-forms. Not unnaturally, a number of schemes have been developed by conservationists to try to combat this problem; schemes which are many and varied in their aims and outlooks. Some involve making it illegal to trade in the products of certain threatened species. Others require the establishment of specially protected areas, where endangered species can be allowed to live in peace. Still others try to address the social and economic issues which cause over-hunting and habitat destruction in the first place. However, in this chapter, I would initially like to concentrate on a very different approach to conservation – that of captive breeding.

The chief proponents of captive breeding – the world's zoos – believe that they have a genuinely important part to play in the battle to stem the tide of extinction. Indeed, some zoos regard captive breeding as being so important that they increasingly offer it as a primary justification for their continued existence, and seek to persuade people of the contribution they can make to the world's conservation efforts. The evidence to support such a view is, however, sorely lacking, as I hope to show.

The zoo man's view of conservation goes something like this. Many species of animal are endangered, and some are more endangered than others. Some are so rare, or are found in habitats that are dwindling so rapidly, that their future survival in the wild can no longer be guaranteed. In such cases, it is argued, the best course of action is to remove them from their natural habitat and transport them to the sheltered environment of zoos, where they can breed without persecution, and slowly build up their numbers. When and if the problems which posed a threat to their existence in the wild are eliminated and the environment is made secure, then numbers of these captive-bred animals can be gradually released: to begin with into a special controlled reserve, and then, all being well, into the wild itself. If the released animals then re-establish themselves in their natural habitat, the mission is branded a success.

At first glance this seems a splendid way to save species and, indeed, as zoos often remind us, it has been highly successful on several occasions. The Hawaiian goose, for instance, was at one time reduced to around thirty examples worldwide. Now it is relatively safe, thanks to the efforts of the Wildfowl Trust at Slimbridge in England and the Pohakuloa breeding centre in Hawaii. The Père David's Deer has been extinct in the wild for over two thousand years but is still in existence because of breeding at Woburn Abbey in England and elsewhere, and a group has been released into Nan Hai Tsu reserve in Beijing (Peking). The Arabian oryx, hunted out of its desert habitat, has recently been returned to Oman and Jordan after captive breeding at San Diego and Phoenix Zoos.

On paper, then, the argument in favour of captive breeding in zoos seems credible. Its object is to save species, and save species it does. However, for such work to be regarded as a valuable contribution to conservation, the rate at which species are rescued through captive breeding would have to come close to or match the rate at which those same species are becoming extinct in the wild. This it patently fails to do.

There are perhaps ten million species of living things thought to be in existence on Earth, of which approximately 45,000 are vertebrates, 250,000 'higher' flowering plants, 100,000 'lower' plants, such as ferns, and the rest invertebrates. Of these, botanists have calculated that one in ten of plant species are threatened with extinction, and zoologists have come up with a similar figure for birds and mammals. If we apply it across the board, and assume it also holds for the invertebrates, then we can deduce that somewhere between 500,000 and one million species are in danger of extinction.

Obviously, it is well beyond the scope of this chapter even to begin to examine every threat to all those endangered species. To do that, I would need to write several books, most of them fairly lengthy. For the purposes of this chapter I will concentrate on just one particular habitat, to illustrate the scale and discuss the effect human activities are having on the area's wildlife. I hope that, in so doing, I will be able to demonstrate just how simplistic it is to assume that zoos can play a significant role in limiting man's destruction. The habitat I have chosen is tropical rainforest.

A recent study by the US National Academy of Sciences estimated that a 10.5 square kilometre area of rainforest might contain 1,500 species of flowering plant, 750 species of tree, 400 of bird, 150 of butterfly, 125 of mammal, 100 of reptile and 60 of amphibian. It proved to be practically

Rainforests – before and after. (Kevin Morgan, The Earthlife Foundation)

impossible to estimate accurately how many insect species there might be in such an area, although a different report suggested that a single hectare could shelter a staggering 42,000 different forms. Approximately one square metre of leaf litter, when examined, yielded 50 species of ant alone.

All in all, such is the wealth of plant and animal life in tropical rainforests that, although they now cover only 2.5 per cent of the planet's surface, they harbour 50 per cent of all its species.

Many of these life-forms are also endemic – that is, they are found in one place only. If, for example, we look at Madagascar's total of 12,000 plant species, we find that over 60 per cent are found nowhere else. What is more, Terry Erwin, of the Smithsonian Institution, has estimated that some unique rainforest plant species support 405 equally unique species of insect. So, in the remarkably rich habitat of the tropical rainforest, the combination of density of species, endemism and rarity means that the destruction of only a comparatively small area can easily lead to the extinction of a great many species. It is sad to report that the world's rainforests are being destroyed, in massive expanses at an alarming rate.

For example, every year thousands of hectares of the rainforests in Central America are cleared so that the land can be converted into pasture for cattle grazing. However, ironically, the cattle are not used to feed the Central Americans themselves. Instead, they suffer the ignominious fate of contributing to the ingredients of hamburgers in the United States. The fast-food chains there use the Central American forests simply because the land is much cheaper than in the USA; and, because it is so cheap, the landowners have no qualms about clearing vast tracts of forest to make way for ludicrously small numbers of cattle, which are often stocked at densities as low as one animal for every five hectares. By employing one man to look after a thousand or more cattle, the cattle barons allow their ranches to support one person per thirty square kilometres. In contrast, by using traditional peasant agriculture, such areas would support between 1,200 and 1,800 people.

Of course, the more beef exported to the American market the less is available for native consumption which, in Central America, has fallen 40 per cent since 1960. Today, the average Costa Rican farmer eats less beef than the average American pet cat.

Rainforests have very thin soils and are poor in nutrients. They only support the seething mass of life they do because of a complex recycling ecology, in which the trees and their associated fungi 'feed' the soil with nutrients just as much as the soil nourishes them. By turning such large areas into pastureland, the cattle-raisers destroy the trees and the fungi. In so doing they also destroy the recycling mechanisms and, ultimately, the ability of the land to support forest in the future. After a couple of years of grazing the whole deforested area becomes susceptible to weeds and disease and proves quite incapable of supporting any more cattle. This is of little concern to the landowners, who simply move their herds elsewhere, but it is a major headache for ecologists, as this form of cattle ranching is depriving

Erosion following logging in Sumatra (Preston Mafham)

us of some 20,000 square hectares of forest every year. As Catherine Caufield observed in *In the Rainforest* (Heinemann, 1985) 'one reason that the Central American rainforests seem doomed to disappear is that their destruction takes five cents off the price of an American hamburger.'

But the ranchers are far from being the only people to accelerate the destruction of rainforests. Every time you or I read a newspaper, write a note, or buy a new piece of furniture – a table, a chair or even a wooden salad bowl – then, as likely as not, we are helping to contribute to the disappearance of the rainforests.

Officially, some 44,000 square kilometres of primary forest are logged for this purpose every year; but records are often misleading, so the true area is probably considerably greater. As with ranching, it is not the scale of the operations that is a cause for concern so much as the methods by which such operations are carried out.

It takes about 150 years for a tropical hardwood tree to grow to maturity. It takes just ten minutes to fell it with chain-saws, and a further 60 seconds to shred the whole trunk into little wooden chips, each about the size of a dollar coin. As the tree falls, the vines and lianas which twine and intertwine, connecting it to other trees in the vicinity, fall with it, and pull other trees to the ground. As the loggers cut down one area of forest at a time, it takes only a few years for entire tracts to be completely destroyed, exposing the soil to the elements and causing the same sort of deterioration as that prompted by the actions of the cattle-ranchers.

The economics of commercial logging are much the same as those of whaling. Both trees and whales take so long to grow to maturity that the only way to make a profit is to take what you can while it is still there.

Consequently, the policy seems to be one of 'take now, pay for it later'. Somewhat ironically, the people who stand to lose most from this arrangement – the native peoples whose very livelihoods would, as we shall see later, be threatened by the disappearance of the forests – are the ones most frequently employed by the logging companies. By being a party to the forests' destruction, such people might be accused of being rather myopic; but Dr Norman Myers, in *The Primary Source* (W. W. Norton, 1984), puts it all into perspective by quoting a Director of Forestry in South East Asia: 'It is not so much that we want to live today, rather than invest in tomorrow. We want to survive today, live a little tomorrow, and think about the future next week!'

This highlights the greatest problem of all in dealing with tropical forest degradation. The inhabitants of the countries which have tropical rainforests are, almost without exception, incredibly poor; and for many of them, working for the loggers – and thus helping to destroy the forests – is their only means of survival.

The tremendous poverty of these people leads directly to another form of deforestation. Because many peasants have no land of their own, they head for where they think they can stake out a claim for themselves. They head for the forest.

For centuries, rainforests have supported subsistence farmers, who survived by shifting cultivation. They cleared a small patch of land, spent a couple of seasons growing rice or cassava, and then, as the soil began to run out of nutrients, they moved on. This was fine when there were only a few shifting cultivators. Now, however, a huge influx of landless peasants is migrating from the towns to the forests. These people have no cultural history as shifting cultivators, and consequently cannot manage the land as effectively as true forest dwellers.

If their numbers remained steady (there are reckoned to be 140 million at present), the future for the forests would look bleak enough, but the human population of rainforest countries is exploding. For example, by the end of the century, Brazil, which currently supports 118.7 million people, will have 176.5 million, increasing to some 281 million by the time the numbers stabilize in the year 2075. Bangladesh – population 90 million at present – will have a staggering 338.2 million people by 2125. The pattern is much the same in other tropical countries. When combined with cattle-raising and commercial logging, this ever-growing population, and the subsequent increase in forest farmers, does not auger well for the world's rainforests.

This wholesale destruction means that about 20 hectares of forest are being felled every minute. Some authorities suggest that as much as two per cent of the biome – the rainforest ecosystem – may be suffering degradation as a result of human activities every year. As a result, many large forest tracts are in peril. Within five years, Australia, Bangladesh, India, Sri Lanka, the Philippines, Thailand, Madagascar, Ecuador, Central America and West and East Africa may be completely devoid of forest, barring that maintained in national parks. The entire Atlantic strip of Amazonia could be gone by the

Timber extraction from tropical rain forest in Borneo. (Glyn Davies/ICCE)

end of the century, as might large areas in Peru, Colombia, the Cameroons, Burma and Papua New Guinea.

It is extremely difficult to say exactly how many species are being lost along the way. Madagascar alone once supported some 200,000 species, most of them in its eastern strip of primary tropical forest. Now 93 per cent of that forest has been destroyed, and, as we know that when a habitat loses 90 per cent of its extent, it also loses half its life forms, it does not seem at all unlikely that Madagascar today is poorer to the tune of some 100,000 species or more. What is more, about 60 per cent of the species are unique to that island, so it may well be that the deforestation of Madagascar has caused up to 60,000 extinctions. Norman Myers, a noted authority on tropical forests, has suggested that it might be not unreasonable to assume that the world is losing one species of living thing every day. Outlandish as it may seem, the available data, supported by several experts, suggests that Myer's estimate might even be on the conservative side.

Viewed in this light, the achievements of zoos somehow look less than impressive. For all the zoos' talk of large-scale captive breeding programmes, even their most ardent admirers would be hard pushed to ascribe to them the credit for saving more than a dozen or so species from extinction – a mere 0.00012 per cent of all the life-forms on earth. Consequently, if we accept Doctor Myers' 'conservative' extinction rate as being reasonably accurate, we can deduce that zoos have, in all probability, saved less species within the last 150 years than have become extinct within the last few days. What is more, no matter what progress they make, what new breeding techniques they learn, and what new technology they develop, they will never be able to increase their success rate sufficiently to preserve in captivity more than a fraction of all the species threatened with extinction in the wild.

The cost of saving species by captive breeding is usually phenomenal. The rescue of the Arabian oryx is reported to have cost $16 million, while it has so far cost $25 million to preserve and breed the Californian condor. In addition it normally requires many, many years of hard work. The first Arabian oryx were released 20 years after the rescue operation began. A century after the first group of Przewalski's horses were captured for zoological collections none have yet been returned to the wild.

To complicate matters further, there are some zoos which, in addition to following the path of 'conservation through captive breeding and rehabilitation' also sense that there might be an opportunity for them to perform a slightly different role. These zoos frequently issue statements to the effect that, such is the rapidity with which the wilderness is disappearing, we can no longer guarantee that any more than the most insignificant scraps will remain. This, some zoos suggest, makes their work all the more valuable, as it means there may come a time when the only remaining specimens of a great many species will be those bred and maintained in zoos. In other words they see the zoo of the future as a living museum, managed by 'knights in shining armour' plucking animals from the path of the bulldozer or forest farmer and preserving them for the benefit of future generations, who would otherwise be denied the opportunity of seeing them.

Like many zoo ideas, this concept seems highly attractive and even respectable – on paper. However, to me it seems illogical, inasmuch as it so clearly contradicts the concept of breeding endangered species in captivity for eventual release into the wild. It seems a peculiarly warped logic of zoos which permits – even eulogizes – the painstaking, time-consuming and costly process of rehabilitating an endangered species into its natural habitat, when the same zoo logic predicts that the habitat is destined to be destroyed anyway.

So, the 'zoo as living museum' argument is inconsistent. In my opinion, it is even irresponsible.

First, it puts entirely the wrong emphasis on conservation. The very concept of plucking animals out of danger suggests that the priority of conservationists is saving animal species whatever the damage being done to the habitat. Once, that might have been so, but today this is a misconception that true conservationists are trying extremely hard to counter. It should be appreciated that if an animal exists on the planet, it has evolved to play a particular role, to fill an ecological niche. If an animal's ecosystem is destroyed, then it no longer has a niche, and although it can be kept alive indefinitely in zoos – put on ice so to speak – there seems little point in doing so.

While zoos continue to put forward this insupportable argument as a justification for their existence, they mislead us all into believing that the worst possible effect of mass habitat destruction is the loss of a few species of exotic animals. Such a belief is not only patently untrue, it could even be

Jaguar on ice. (Fanny Dubes)

described as dangerous, for what the zoos fail to mention is that, by allowing the rainforests to disappear, we would do more than witness mass extinctions. We would also be directly responsible for the starvation and even death of millions of our fellow human beings. Tucked away in our cosy surburban dwellings, it is easy for us to forget that, amongst the four to five million species that depend on the rich rainforest environment for their survival, there are human representatives as well. There is a great deal of irony in this situation. It is ironic that the people who need the rainforests to survive, by their own actions – prompted by the insatiable demands of the developed world – are causing those selfsame forests to die.

It is not an exaggeration to say that, should the forests vanish completely, the very livelihoods of those who rely on them will disappear too. For without the complex recycling ecology of the forest, the soil on which the subsistence farmers and others depend will soon become barren, and millions of people will face starvation. We are all distressingly familiar with the tragic pictures of refugees in Ethiopia and the Sudan, but how many are aware that deforestation was as much to blame as the drought and civil war? Should tropical deforestation in other countries continue to spiral out of control, then what is happening in Africa today could take place elsewhere with alarming regularity.

A number of other local environmental factors must also be considered. Under normal conditions, much of the water that falls onto rainforests is breathed back into the atmosphere through a process known as evapotranspiration. When the forest is felled, this does not happen, rain falls less frequently, rivers dry up and drought ensues. Ironically, however, when

the rain does come it brings flooding.

During a heavy rainstorm a tropical forest acts as a sponge: the rain falls into the canopy, trickling down branches or descending in a fine mist so that by the time it reaches the ground it has been dissipated and partly absorbed by the leaves of the trees. But take the forest cover away, and rain falls uninterrupted with full force onto the thin, fragile layer of earth. The soil is washed into the rivers, turning them into torrents of mud.

The effects of rainforest loss are not solely limited to the inhabitants of the immediate area. Half the protein in the world today is derived from rainforest-descended crops, and although most of these foodstuffs are now grown in plantations, they frequently need infusion of genetic material from their wild relations to maintain their productivity, to improve their taste and to bolster their resistance to different diseases.

The forests may even yield completely new foods. The winged bean, for example, which is a plant from the forests of New Guinea, is said to rival the soyabean for nutritional value. Already it is helping to improve the lot of people in 50 tropical nations. There are also natural sweeteners, one of which, a berry from West Africa, rejoicing in the delightful name of *Dioscoreophyllum cuminsii*, is three thousand times sweeter than sucrose, and far less fattening.

Perhaps even more promising than these resources are the myriad medicines that lie concealed in the forests' interior. Because the tropics contain a lot of species in a very small area, there is understandably a great deal of competition between them. As most are immobile, like plants, or only moderately mobile, like some insects, they cannot escape predation by flight or attack. Instead, many turn to chemical warfare as a 'means of defence',

Hundreds more major drugs could still be discovered in tropical rainforest flora. (Mark Boulton/ICCE)

and fortunately for us some of the chemicals produced, far from being harmful, are positively beneficial to humans.

For example, a poison with which Amazonian Indians used to kill people is now used by surgeons as an anaesthetic, without which delicate operations like tonsillectomies and abdominal surgery would be more difficult. Rauwolfia, a product of the snakeroot plant, makes life easier for sufferers from high blood pressure, hypertension and schizophrenia. Thanks to two alkaloids in a tiny, attractive flower called the Rosy periwinkle, a child with leukaemia, who only twenty years ago might have had a mere one in five chance of living to maturity, is now four times as likely to survive. And so it goes on.

Only one in ten of tropical forest plants have been screened for possible medicinal benefit, and only one in a hundred screened intensively. Judging from previous results, we may yet discover another eight hundred major drugs in tropical rainforest flora.

More important, however, than all these considerations is the function of tropical forests as regulators of the Earth's climate. Rainforests contain about half the carbon found in the biota (the world's living things). When forests are felled and burned, in the course of clearing a patch of land for cattle ranchers or for subsistence farming, some of that carbon is released into the air.

This carbon then combines with atmospheric oxygen to form carbon dioxide gas, which is partly responsible for a phenomenon known as the 'greenhouse effect'. Simply, this means that some of the heat and light, normally reflected off our planet's surface, is trapped, heating the earth. A little warmth is essential but too much can prove positively disastrous.

If, for example, the levels of carbon dioxide in the atmosphere were twice what they are today, then average global temperatures would probably be warmer than at any time since dinosaurs ruled the earth. Such temperatures would almost certainly cause a significant melting of the Arctic icecaps, at least in the summer months. This in turn would lead to flooding and great coastal cities such as London, Los Angeles, New York, San Francisco, Montreal and Amsterdam would all face devastation.

Rainfall patterns would be severely disrupted. The wheat-growing industry of the United States would be decimated. But the formerly desert areas of the Islam world would become amongst the most fertile places on earth. There would most certainly be a significant number of local wars breaking out at regular intervals over disputes concerning natural resources.

If all this sounds like science-fiction, then consider the evidence produced by a recently published report. It showed that, not only is the earth becoming warmer, but that this warming corresponds with an increase in the build-up of atmospheric carbon dioxide. Scare-mongering? Unlikely. The report was published by the U. S. Department of Energy.

Talk of the 'greenhouse effect', of famine, of flooding and of medicine is, of course, much removed from the captive-breeding programmes undertaken by zoos. But it does, I hope, go no small way towards showing that conservation should no longer be considered solely as an animal problem, which is how zoos like to present it. Rather, it should be regarded as a solution – a human solution – to a human problem. Perhaps one day, someone, somewhere will show me a zoo that can provide a home for several million species and a livelihood for just as many people, a zoo that can protect against landslides, flooding and drought, that can cure a child of cancer and regulate the earth's climate. Should that day ever dawn, I will look upon zoos in a different light. But until then, I shall remain firm in my conviction that saving the wild is the only practical means of conservation.

Happily, despite claims to the contrary by some zoos, this is still not beyond us. For example, if we stay with our theme of deforestation, we can see that there is much which can be done to help the inhabitants of tropical nations, while easing the burden on their forests.

For example, as the profit on processed wood is between five and twenty times greater than the profit on the raw material, by encouraging local people to process more of their own wood, prior to export, there will be a greater incentive for them to manage their forests carefully for future use.

Logging methods can also be changed. Already some companies – such as PICOP in the Philippines – have tried what is known as 'selective logging'. The theory behind this is that only trees above a certain size are logged, with the smaller ones being left unharmed. The loggers then move off to a different area, and in the years that follow, the untouched trees protect the soil and eventually grow to maturity, at which time the loggers return and begin the cycle again. Theoretically, this means that an area of forest can be harvested indefinitely with only minimal ecological disturbance. In practice, however, things tend to be different; the roads which are built to provide access to the logging areas, and the haphazard methods of tree-felling mean that 60 per cent of the uncut trees are damaged, often fatally. At the same time, the weight of bulldozers squeezes air out of the soil, making it impossible for life to gain a foothold in the future. For this reason, cynics have come to define selective logging as 'selecting an area of forest, and logging it'.

The principle of selective logging is not without hope, however. In steep terrain in Central Borneo, trees are extracted by helicopters. In the short-term, this is expensive, but over a long period it would prove its worth through the number of trees it would save. It has even been suggested that we need no longer exploit untouched forests in the course of commercial logging activities. Where forests manage to regrow in areas that have been logged, they are called 'secondary forests' and are invariably less rich, biologically, than their predecessors. Norman Myers is amongst those who have suggested that, with proper management procedures, secondary forests could supply us with all the industrial wood we need from the tropics until the year 2000.

The predicament of forest farmers might well be solved by a concept known as agroforestry. This involves encouraging the farmer to plant certain species of leguminous trees at the same time as he sows his crops, such as tea, coffee, bananas and corn. The trees provide the soil with nitrogenous nutrients, and at the same time produce domestic wood, industrial timber and paper pulp. By the time the farmer is ready to move elsewhere, his trees should restore forest cover to the area.

Of course, this would be an expensive project. In fact, the United Nations Food and Agriculture Organization (FAO) has estimated the implementation of schemes such as these would require approximately $8 billion a year for a decade or more. It is to be hoped that much of this sum would be met by the private sector and by governments of the Third World countries themselves; leaving the developed nations to find just one billion dollars or so a year. It sounds a lot of money until it is put in perspective. Even being highly pessimistic and allowing for two million of the estimated five million tropical forest species to become extinct, that annual billion dollars works out at only about $350 per species. This compares most favourably with the $25 million dollars spent so far on the Californian condor. Of course, this evaluation does not even consider the environmental, medicinal and climatic services rainforests have to offer.

Spread amongst the inhabitants of the developed world, this equates to 63 cents per head of population. Not much to ask, considering how much is at stake. Put another way, it is equivalent to what the world spends on armaments in twelve hours. I cannot see Armageddon breaking out in half a day – and indeed, given that many conflicts are triggered by disputes over natural resources, conservation could even help ease the tension in some areas. We spend $750 billion every year on weapons designed to end life.

Running for a better future – Sportaid. (Unicef 86)

Could we not find it within ourselves to spend a fraction of that amount on measures designed to preserve and improve life? It seems so little to ask.

Were the world run by people with common sense, then protection of the environment would be amongst the top priorities of every country on earth. But the world is run by politicians. Consequently, progress on such issues is often painfully slow.

It is perhaps uncharitable of me, but I frequently get the impression that a government will only finance an operation if its benefits (a) make a contribution to the donor country's gross national product or (b) are felt in time for the next general election. Pouring money into the likes of forest conservation in the Third World tends to satisfy neither criterion, and so environmental projects such as these have often been shelved. Until recently, this was of little consequence, as none of the people the politicians claimed to represent really cared about rainforests either. Now, slowly but surely, that is beginning to change. Issues such as deforestation are beginning to affect the collective public consciousness, and there are some sectors of the community which are becoming quite concerned about the destruction of the environment. Nowhere is this concern more deeply felt than among young people.

The youth of the world get an unfair Press. To the popular tabloids, we are evidently nothing more than a collection of poorly-educated, ill-mannered renegades, hell-bent on anarchy and total destruction, and deserving of regular doses of flogging, hanging, eye-gouging and what have you, to bring us into line. Needless to say, I reject this attitude. Whilst not denying that there are several unsavoury traits in today's youth which have not always been present, I would most strongly challenge the way in which the media – and the older generation – look at the past through rose-tinted spectacles. As somebody once said, the good old days are a combination of a very bad memory and an overactive imagination.

No, there is a lot more to my generation than some would have us believe. Indeed, I suspect that the true picture is radically different from that so often painted. Like most young people throughout modern history, the youth of today are on the whole more liberal, more open-minded in their attitude than the previous generation. They often see injustices where their parents see normality. When the outgoing generation excuse such injustices on the grounds that 'it has always been so', there are often young people who ask 'But why has it? And need it be so in the future?'

In this sense, the attitude of today's youth is much the same as that of their elders when they too were young. But it would be wrong to assume that they are carbon copies of previous generations; on the contrary, there have been a number of developments in society as a whole which make the disaffection of today's young people a different matter entirely from that of their forebears.

Firstly, young people are far more aware of world events. Within the last few decades, the mass media concept has well and truly arrived, so that anyone can flick a switch on 'the box' and bring pictures of war, famine, environmental destruction and similar such disturbing images from across the world into their living room. Secondly, these images are supported by a plethora of specialist publications from organizations which give much more accurate information than the limited, and often biased, news coverage. Lastly, many of today's young find that they are facing an uncertain future. Unemployment in the United Kingdom may be paradise compared to the life of a forest-farmer in Costa Rica, but for many it is a sufficiently bleak experience to stir up dissatisfaction with a world that can seem cold and uncaring – a world, furthermore, in whose creation young people had no say.

All of these factors combine to create a concerned generation keen to change the world for the better. Of course, this is not to say that everyone under 25 is wracked with grief over the continued destruction of the environment. Indeed, for the majority such issues probably do not merit more than a moment's thought. There is nothing new in this: throughout history, most people have gone through life without particularly strong opinions on anything, leaving it to a dedicated but vocal minority to get things done. However, what is especially encouraging about this new generation is that the minority is increasing all the time, becoming more vocal as it does so. That can only be a change for the better, for it is the determination and the positive attitude of young people that is the main hope of averting the environmental crisis we all face.

Bill Travers

'Inadmissible Evidence'

Bill Travers, born in Northumberland, had intended to become a doctor, but his studies were interrupted by the war. He served in the Far East with the Gurkhas and Wingate, and was eventually seconded to SOE and parachuted into Malaya to help organize Chinese resistance. Returning to England after six years, he wrote film scripts and, after a period in repertory, played in several West End shows. He appeared in a number of films, including *Geordie*, *The Smallest Show on Earth*, *Ring of Bright Water* and *Born Free*, before writing and directing/producing wildlife documentaries for his own company – also in association with Oxford Scientific Films, Hugo van Lawick, Jane Goodall and Simon Trevor.

Sir Frank Fraser Darling, an outstanding naturalist, believes that in some respects we can only decipher an animal's world if we resort to human vocabulary.

There were several families on the hillside that sunny morning gathering food. Their chatter and laughter mingled with the sounds of wind through the trees and faded into the thunder of a far-off cascade of water. Advancing on the track leading to the hillside were several men armed with rifles, ropes and sticks. Some paused to look in her direction then hurried on, fanning out, making as little noise as possible. The mother turned to face the

The mother turned to face the intruder . . . (Bill Travers)

intruders. The rest turned to form a half circle. Shots rang out and echoed across the hills. They turned screaming and shouting in confusion and fear.

But she stood, too petrified to move – robbed of all action by fear and watched figures of the white men and black men as they forged a path towards her.

Only when the sounds of her friends and family faded, echoing in the forest, did she realize that the mottled carpet of shade had swallowed up fleeing mothers and their offspring, her play-friends, and now she was standing alone.

'They look so strange – why are they coming towards me, nearer and nearer. Everyone is running, it is not a game I play with the others. Where are my friends I was playing with . . . where is my mother. Oh, I do not understand . . . I am very frightened.

'I must run but my legs are wobbling and bending, I cannot control them. I cannot see my mother anywhere – they are coming right behind me . . . I cannot breathe – where do I go – where are the others . . . Oh, I am falling . . . I must get up. I am being dragged down.'

East African Standard 2 November 1968
She was caught on August 20 at Darajani, near Mtito Andei, by Mr Ken Stewart. (An animal trapper).

Pole Pole in the trapper's compound outside Nairobi. (Bill Travers)

'I am still alive, I cannot move, even when I struggle I can see them all above me looking down. Their faces tell me they are happy and strong, they shout.

'I must escape somehow.

'Yes . . . yes I can – I can make the noise, the shouting go – I can go back . . . It is becoming better, I can go to my mother . . . I can smell her milk and I can suck as she strokes my head and lingeringly touches, caresses me . . . I will never wake up.

Iain and Oria Douglas-Hamilton's *Among the Elephants*
For elephants, the unity of a family is one of the most important things in their lives. I was deeply moved by the constant affection and care which they showed every day within the families; mothers, daughters, sisters, babies all touching and communicating with each other in a very loving way.

'I bump up and down as the ground moves under me. My side hurts as it rubs against the wood and the ropes bite into my legs. I can see the trees above me as I travel across the sky.'

Time Out 13 May 1983 (Andrew Tyler)
After her capture, Pole was taken to a trapper's compound outside Nairobi.

'Why is there no one else. I must go back into my happiness . . . my dreams.

'The sun is disappearing and everything is quite still – I am still. I am somewhere else. Everything smells so different. That is what is frightening. I should go back again – in my mind – where it is safe, but I have to look . . . I am curious.

'I see thick bars everywhere as thick as bamboo, bars as thick as trees. They are all around me.

'How strange, I am quite alone but I cannot do anything except walk a few paces.

'There is some water and food . . . I must have been dreaming when I arrived . . . it is growing dark, the orange sun has turned red the edges of my prison bars, red – red-brown and burnt like the red of the soil on the hillside, like the dust that we wear on our skin.

'Nearly every day now they come to look at me. They all looked the same at first – like the people who caught me. But now I can recognize some, especially those who are a little afraid of me. I think I would like to hurt them . . . I am afraid of some of them.

'It is best at night. I can hear the voices of the other prisoners and, even though I cannot understand their language, I know sometimes what they are saying, especially when they are afraid. They talk all the time of death and smell of fear. It is what everyone thinks about – what will happen next. What will it be like to die.

'It is difficult to find somewhere to avoid their eyes – I can manage if I put my forehead against a post. That is how I stand.

'Today there are different sounds. Everyone is very excited. There is quite a different scent in the air. Suddenly I am being urged to go this way and that – I am being prodded and forced into a little prison at the end of my run.'

Time Out 13 May 1983 (Andrew Tyler)
Here she was crated ready for her next destination. There was some confusion as to what this was intended to be. The *Born Free* actors, Bill Travers and Virginia McKenna, heard about her and were told that she had already been gifted to London Zoo by President Kenyatta. They asked if her departure might be delayed so they might use her in their movie *An Elephant Called Slowly* which was being shot in the south of the country at Tsavo National Park; Travers and McKenna's request was granted.

'The worst thing is this prison moves. Soon the home I have known for the past few nights has disappeared in the trees.

'Everything rushes past me faster and faster . . . much faster than I can run . . . faster than I can see. I fight to escape . . . but I cannot escape my bars . . .

Time Out 13 May 1983 (Andrew Tyler)
Daphne Sheldrick, widow of the former chief warden of Tsavo, remembers

David Sheldrick and Pole Pole. (Colin Jobson)

Pole arriving for filming 'tense and bewildered' on the back of a lorry. Her spread, in inhospitable bush land, was already base camp to numerous orphaned beasts, such as rhinos, buffaloes, ostriches and more elephants, all of whom mixed in with each other in a raucous but generally co-operative fashion.

'In my big open prison I stand. In cool shade under a tree. I think I hate these people. Now I must escape, my hatred makes me stronger.

'But I am worried . . . I do not feel that these people hate me . . . they offer me fresh fruit which I love to eat but I am afraid when they try to come near me. They try to touch me. I lash out to hurt them – to kill them if I can.

'They do not seem to understand, they always come back with soft caresses and sweet fruit . . . and I hate them . . . and they are gentle, trying to caress me.

'What do they want . . . if only I could understand them. If only I could hear their thoughts.'

Time Out 13 May 1983 (Andrew Tyler)

Pole, Sheldrick reports, charged everything in range. But within two days her husband David had quietened the elephant and on the fourth she was ready for film work.

I rush across my prison, my mother is there – tall, magnificent . . . she stretches over the bars.
(Colin Jobson)

Oh yes, and I do not live in a prison any more. (Colin Jobson)

'I rush across my prison, my mother is there – tall, magnificent . . . she stretches over the bars . . . but it is not my mother. I stop in horror. I am very frightened. But she is so like my mother and she talks to me softly and quietly . . . rumbling the words deeply in her belly.

'I wonder if I am right to trust these people.

'Kind now, but what will they do to me tomorrow. I let them come in my prison but I am frightened . . . I let them touch me. They are not afraid and when I rush at them they do not run, they pat me . . . they make funny, almost happy sounds even when I have knocked them down.

'Oh, it is such fun, we play games all day long. These strange people like me I tell myself . . . well, they seem to like to be with me all the time. Oh yes, and I do not live in a prison any more, that is in the day time I mean. Of course, we all wander into our prisons at night, you see there is lots of food there.

'We can eat all night long. Playing so much during the day makes me very hungry . . . there is no time to eat.

'Eleanor is sixteen years old. She is really a mother to me and to the others. She likes to caress me.

'It is really strange, we have so many different shaped friends and practically everyone has a different language, although of course, we can communicate . . . I mean we can all say what we are feeling, though not so much to people, however hard we try.

'Quite a lot of the people have suddenly disappeared. It is much quieter. I go for long walks with the others. Everybody feels that something is going to happen soon.'

East African Standard 2 November 1968
She impressed everybody on the set with her good nature and acting ability.

Time Out 13 May 1983 (Andrew Tyler)
Filming over, the actors flew to President Kenyatta's residence outside Nairobi for an evening of movie watching. McKenna says she opened her mouth to beg the release of Pole back into the wild but stopped short, knowing the President had already favoured them by delaying the departure and that, if not Pole, another infant would have to be caught in her place.

'All my friends, my new family . . . especially Eleanor . . . are strange today . . . more loving than ever I have known. I know they are saying goodbye. I can see the little prison I arrived in.

'Perhaps I am going home . . . perhaps I am going somewhere beautiful . . . to a hillside . . . . . . home. I must not cry . . . I must try to remember all the happiness I have known these past few weeks.'

Letter to Bill Travers and Virginia McKenna from Mrs Daphne Sheldrick, wife of Senior Game Warden of Tsavo National Park 5 December 1968
The Park [Tsavo] is looking so beautiful now. The rains have started and the country is green and carpeted with flowers. The game, all look so well and fat

We got the animal second hand from their wretched film. (Colin Jobson)

and full of the joy of living. Our own orphans adore the rains, and Pole Pole too experienced a little of this joy when a heavy shower fell just before she had to leave. She and the others rolled and frolicked in the mud for hours, and were so obviously enjoying themselves that it was a pleasure to watch. We felt like traitors, knowing that this was the only opportunity poor little Pole Pole would ever have to be really at home. Incidentally, Eleanor especially and to a lesser extent Kadenge, were terribly upset when Pole Pole left. Eleanor tried to climb out of the stockade to go to Pole Pole's rescue, and reach out her trunk to fondle Pole Pole and try to pull her back as she walked past. There is no doubt that they missed her very much for a few days.

The Observer 3 November 1968
Kenya has presented a two-and-a-half year old female elephant, Pole Pole, Swahili for slowly, to London Zoo to replace Diksie, a Kenyan elephant who died after an accident last year.

Daily Mail 7 February 1983
Doctor David Jones, a veterinary surgeon and Assistant Director at London Zoo, says 'we got the animal second-hand from their wretched film. After film work was completed there was no way the elephant could be returned to the wild, so the Kenyan government presented it to us.'

'I am back in my little prison in Nairobi. I often think of Eleanor . . . . .

I can almost feel her soft trunk brushing my head.

'Some people came to see me today . . . my little prison, the one I travel in, is near my little playground.

'Where am I going. Why can't I just be left to wander on the hillside with my mother or Eleanor.'

East African Standard 2 November 1968

AN ELEPHANT STAR TURNS ENVOY

The diplomats, one recently arrived to take up his post in Kenya, the other just leaving to take up hers in Britain, met at an unusual ceremony at Kabete yesterday.

One was the new British High Commissioner in Kenya, Mr Eric Norris . . . the other was Pole Pole a two-and-a-half year old elephant who is giving up a film star's life for that of an envoy. She was given her diplomatic rank by the Minister of Tourism and Wildlife, Mr Ayodo, who presented her to Mr Norris as a gift from the President and the government to London Zoo. He described her as an ambassador of goodwill and hoped she would make many friends in Britain and show them some of the charms of Kenya. Diplomatic exchanges were complete when Pole Pole accepted a banana from Mr Norris.

'They gave me some leaves . . . and a banana.'

The Observer 3 November 1968

Pole Pole is to be flown to London on November 12.

London Zoo's elephant house, designed by Sir Hugh Casson. (Ian Dobbie)

Time Out 13 May 1983 (Andrew Tyler)
The habitat itself was a towering concrete structure topped by numerous cone shapes, designed by the celebrated Sir Hugh Casson . . . During the night Pole was chained inside one of six pens.

One occupant was Rusty, who was to die the following year. Another was Lakshmi, a large and increasingly temperamental Asian, who carried children on her back until she ran wild towards a tunnel . . . the third, a fellow African (elephant) was called Toto.

'It is *very* cold and the air smells damp and stale and acrid . . . All the smells are different; but stranger than anything else, I can sense the awful stench of death.

'There are always some prisoners dying and their sick and diseased breath settles on everything . . . infecting it . . . so that even the trees and grass smell sour.'

The Zoological Society of London 1979–1981 Scientific Report – Pathology
During the period from the 1 January to the 1 December 1979 inclusive, a total of 889 post mortem examinations was carried out. Fifty-five domestic animals were examined and the non-domestic animals were divided into 401 Mammalia, 245 Aves, 149 Reptilia, 14 Amphibia and 25 Pisces.

In the collection at Regent's Park, carcasses examined, excluding those of domesticated species, numbered 623.

'This is a real prison – all grey concrete and huge iron bars. Why must I live in a prison? Eleanor has never lived in a prison. There are three prisoners here like myself who speak my language. Rusty, she has beautifully short ears and comes from India; Toto, she is about sixteen and came from Zambia when she was only one year old. Her parents and her family were all shot as they gathered round her she says. Lakshmi is the youngest, another beautiful Indian.

'But why are we here? What have we all done? What a strange place. There are hundreds of other prisoners – prisoners from all countries of the world – and together they make a strange wailing sound, talking of their fears, hopelessness, frustration; some are still crying for their loved ones. The little ones – the children – are sitting in corners bewildered.

'Why are we here . . . what have we done . . . The noise is terrible, but it seems the wardens in their uniforms cannot hear these terrible sounds or feel the unhappiness. They do not appear to hear anything. I think they cannot imagine the suffering.'

The Daily Express 20 October 1983
John Knowles, who runs the 118-acre Marwell Zoological Park in Hampshire, maintains . . . 'I do not believe, in a zoo that is well-run, that animals are unhappy. If you want to be sentimental about it, their lives are probably better than they might be in the wild.'

Private Eye 26 September 1980
Knowles made his fortune from intensive poultry farming, an industry not best famous for recommending itself to animal-lovers.

'Shortly after it gets light the prison visitors arrive, they bring little bags of food, some they eat themselves some they give to us. They laugh mostly but beneath their laughter there are some with feelings of real sorrow. I can see it in their eyes. It is almost as if they could hear, could understand some of our language. Sometimes we can communicate our feelings with our eyes. Sometimes the prison visitors are very sad but they seldom cry.

'It is strange . . . we are all three the same shape . . . but we are not a family . . . I do not talk much any more to my three friends. I think of my mother, Eleanor, and those few weeks of happiness. Within these memories I build my dreams. I live in my dreams. If I do not, my imprisonment and my innocence is not acceptable. For me there cannot any longer be reality. I stand and rock from one foot to another, I can rock myself into a dream world. I rock more and with the same rhythms I can travel further and further down, deep into my past.

I stand and rock from one foot to another.
I can rock myself into a dream world.
(Ian Dobbie)

Letter to Bill Travers and Virginia McKenna from Mrs Daphne Sheldrick, wife of Senior Game Warden of Tsavo National Park dated 5 December 1968
It was extremely good of you to write and give us news of Pole Pole, who, I can assure you, has been very much in our thoughts the past weeks. We too are so sorry that she had to go, she would have been happy in Tsavo with the others, but then, if Pole Pole had been spared, another baby would have to take her place, so there really was no solution. Like you though, the thought of life imprisonment, especially for an animal like an elephant that loves the wide open spaces, fills me with such sorrow that it doesn't do to think about, and I'm sure the film series that you both have embarked on will do a lot to make people see the injustice of zoos.

'I pace up and down, I see and hear no one. The same paces, feet in the same places . . . . I am travelling back to when I was born. I emerge all wet, dripping from the soft black earth . . . . . It is wonderful . . . . I see myself on a hillside in bright sunshine gathering sweet smelling wild grasses and flowers . . . . . . I am in a valley, everything is green. I wander under the bright green leaves in the fresh air, in the cool fresh water of the mountain streams and along the banks to gather sweet tasting fruits. Oh, the taste of sweet gathered fruits . . . I bit the warder's thumb. He put his hand in my mouth.
'I reel back. I am hit by a stick and made to go into my cell. The fruit-bearing branches of my beautiful trees spread out and turn into grey iron bars. The happy bird song in my ears is distorted into the metallic screech of shutting iron doors. The murmuring of the wind in the trees grows louder and louder into the moans of an approaching meat wagon, and the sweet echoing calls of my forest grow more shrill in my head and turn into the shrieks and outraged yells of many prisoners who can endure their helplessness and the boredom of their captivity no longer.'

The Observer 23 October 1983
Desmond Morris, former Curator of Mammals, says – 'the present set-up at Regent's Park is out-of-date. We now know that animals must be kept in carefully designed enclosures and given expert care. Otherwise, they will suffer and die. If you keep an animal confined you must give it something in return . . . an interesting environment, the companionship of others and proper health care,' he says. 'It is just not on to stick them in cages and leave them.'

'I try to be sane, to accept the grim reality. I try to think of something to say to my friends but they are just prisoners like me, not my family really, and there is hardly anything to say – nothing happens . . . . . they inhabit their dreams . . . I cringe in mine. That is the worst part. Nothing happens. It is not living, it is watching something die . . . yourself. What is there left to say. It is a living death. Soon you do not care, there are none of the many grasses we have to leave the forest for – the sweet and sharp tasting herbs we need. We do not have the adventure of searching for them, or the fun and excitement of finding them and picking what we want or what we need. Men in uniforms are given stuff for us to eat. It really is just *stuff*. Maybe the

It's just not on to stick them in cages and leave them .
(Bill Travers)

doctors in the white house know what prisoners should eat each day, just how much, how little, to keep healthy . . . to keep alive, but still there are hundreds of deaths.'

The Zoological Society of London 1979–1981 Scientific Report – Bacterial Infections
As in most years, approximately twenty per cent of all deaths in acclimatized animals were associated with disease due to bacteria.

'It is very dangerous to get ill. The big bosses in the white building see that no one is allowed to become disabled or crippled or very old. They have the answer for everything. If you become ill you are given "The Big S", at least that is what they say.

'Someone said "S" is for syringe, but I do not know what that is . . . I suppose I will find out one day . . . I am sorry I have been rude and unpleasant. It is just that I am frightened when I am not living in my dreams . . . I wonder if all prisoners dream the same dreams . . .

'There has been a lot going on over the past two years in the way of comings and goings. Rusty has gone. She is dead. No one seems to know how. The prisoners talk a lot but no one is sure. We could tell she was dead from the breeze when it blew past her cell, and we gathered near the door and put our heads against the metal. I think Toto and Lakshmi and I were friends for a brief moment – maybe we were frightened – I do not think any of us really knows what death is like or what it means. But after that we crept back inside ourselves. Toto does not like me. She is chained up inside a lot of the time and I am locked outside for the prison visitors to look at. I think it is because I stole Toto's toy, a rubber tyre, and she hit me, so I bit her.

'I wish they would stop looking at me and holding out their hands. Their eyes are not cruel, in fact they look kind, but apart from throwing things that I am supposed to eat – silly things like peanuts or stones – they never do anything . . . they just watch and talk and laugh. It is odd, sometimes they give me round pieces of metal. What can I do with them – I tried to eat them at first. Toto once ate an umbrella I am told.'

East African Standard 2 November 1968
Mr Ayodo (Kenya's Minister of Wildlife and Tourism) said his Ministry was always careful to ensure that zoo conditions for Kenyan animals were of the best and he was happy that Pole Pole would be living in the new pavilion.

The Zoological Society of London 1979–1981 Scientific Report – Accidents and Injuries
As usual, injuries made up a significant portion of the causes of death in some groups of mammals, notably rodents, primates and ungulates.

'There is one vistor who comes and sits and looks at me, even when it is very cold . . . she sits for hours just looking. I can see her eyes are wet even though she smiles at me. I try to talk to her but she cannot hear the sounds I make.'

We could tell she was dead from the breeze when it blew past her cell . . . I am locked outside. (Ian Dobbie)

Sunday Times 3 October 1982 (Brian Jackman)
THREE TONS OF LONELINESS
'Being the national collection, it would be very unrepresentative if we did not have elephants at Regents Park.' (David Jones, current Senior Veterinary Officer at the Zoo).

Daily Express 24 October 1983
YOU EXPRESS YOUR VIEWS
'Any living creature deprived of freedom must, like Pole Pole, suffer mental cruelty . . . Nothing humans or animals do can cope with enforced inactivity. Perhaps now something will be done for the mental health of these wonderful, patient creatures.' Kenneth Quicke, Wilmington, East Sussex.

'One of the warders was pushing something up inside Toto. They are always pushing things up where we piss from. He was very nervous and he was almost killed – trampled on and speared by Toto's big long teeth. They do not seem to know what hurts us and what does not . . . what is painful . . . what we like or cannot stand . . . what is driving us mad . . . and we cannot tell them. The warders are strange, some of them even love us but they do not know anything really. We hear them speaking but they cannot hear us. I think that is why we get chained up.'

The Times 19 October 1983
AN ELEPHANT'S UNHAPPY LIFE
Part of the explanation for Pole Pole's unhappy existence at the zoo was that she had not been trained, Mr Jones said. 'When she first came to us there was a move not to train animals too much.' As a result she was less adaptable and more difficult to handle.

Daily Express 19 October 1983
David Jones, the Zoo's Assistant Director and chief vet, said: 'We would rather not keep elephants at all. But seventy per cent of the visiting public says an elephant is a necessary part of the visit to the zoo.'

The Daily Express 21 October 1983 (George Gale)
Stuff 'the public'. If 'the public' that insists on keeping elephants in zoos had its way, we would still be throwing Christians to lions.

'To be a prisoner with no hope of release – ever, kept in a yard, chained in a concrete cell – I cannot describe the feeling. But there is a worse feeling starting in my head. When finally you find nothing to love, you live with hatred. With only hatred for all, a second, far worse inner prison is created inside your mind, and you withdraw, brooding . . . burning.
   'I find myself hating and I hate myself and rock from side to side for hours saying no . . . no . . . no. . . . No, I must stop thinking about myself – but what else is there . . . except to rock and search for dreams.'

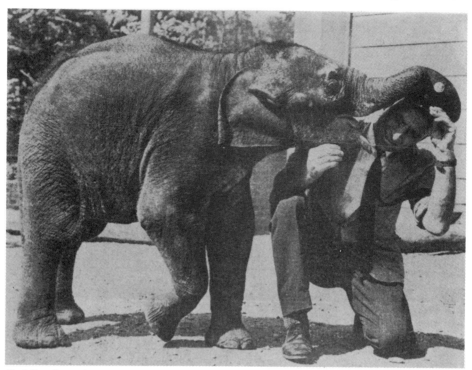

Cuddles for sad Anna to make her forget.   (Evening News, 23 June 1970)

'Today is full of breathless hope . . . all sorts of news from other prisoners. Suddenly I see leaves, trees, sky. I hear the birds calling, warning, replying. I am *not* dreaming. Today is special – very very special. A friend is coming, one of us – a baby . . . a little baby just six months old. Oh, I will love her. We will go away together to the hillside where I was born . . .

'She has arrived and she is being fed on bottles of milk by the nice warder, the one I like. She is beautiful – I long to touch her. She is very small – she has a name, Anna of Siam . . . Oh, I am so happy . . . and sad . . . I am suddenly sad . . . I start to think . . . She's just a baby . . . Why is she a prisoner?

'Where is her mother. Did her mother turn and run off in to the forest like my mother . . . I think my mother did not run off really. I think that when the shots rang out she died . . . they killed her. But I cannot say she is dead. If I want Anna to be with me it is because I am lonely. I need her but I do not think she needs me – or any of us, with our hatred . . . except, I suppose, she will soon.

'It starts off fine but each week, each month, year, a little bit of eggshell peels off the world leaving only a transparent skin between you and the red jelly of your butchered carcass. I know . . . The other prisoners tell me what happens . . .

'Must not think, just be cheerful. She must not see me sad . . .Anna.'

Letter to the Director of London Zoo from Mrs Daphne Sheldrick 18 July 1982

My late husband, David, was warden of the giant Tsavo National Park in Kenya for thirty years until the time of his death, and he was probably the greatest authority that ever lived on elephants, both wild and tame. In Tsavo during his time there was a population of 35,000 wild elephants, and over the years many orphaned calves were brought in to us. We reared them, cared for them and rehabilitated them back to the wild state, so I think I, too, can claim to know a little about elephants . . . I am sure I do not need to tell you that elephants are thinking, caring animals of extremely high intelligence; sensitive feeling creatures with VERY long memories. In the natural state they are the most gentle and sociable of all animals – strangers are accepted into a herd, babies are adopted and different herds mingle peaceably and freely at watering and feeding places, without rancour. Their society, as you know, is matriarchal, the females forming lasting life-long bonds of friendship and loyalty. They need the companionship, love and security of a closely knit elephant family, and Pole Pole is no exception.

If she is difficult, aggressive and vicious, then there is a good reason for it, for elephants, under normal circumstances are not naturally so . . .

'I had a long talk with Anna this morning. Her mother was not killed when she was sent here, she says. I said that I thought my mother ran off into the forest, but I know she would never have left me. Anna is very gentle and kind and she makes me laugh which is wonderful. When she gets excited her ears flap wildly and she bounces up and down with her two front feet together. It makes me so happy to see her. It is so good to laugh again. She gently touches my face with her trunk. I remember I touched my mother's face and her breasts and her lovely body just like that. She told me about the outside world, about tall trees and what she ate and the smells of the forest she knew. It sounded so like my home at times that I had to stop her, and I went away and stood with my head against an iron post and cried to myself for all the rest of that day. I do not think the warders can hear us when we cry.

I heard today from other prisoners how Rusty died. They say she was put to sleep so that the men from the white house could look at her backside or feet. No-one seems to know exactly what they did. They never say – but they killed her. It was very simple. They shot her. People in the white house do not want the prison visitors to know what really happens here in prison. Of course, everyone knows that Rajah was shot because he badly hurt his warder. Perhaps his warder should not have thrashed him so hard for taking sweets and pennies from the children of prison visitors. Perhaps he couldn't take another beating . . .

'We should be thankful to be alive. I am. Other prisoners are killed almost every week. There are hundreds of deaths every year. I can never get used to the smell of death. When animals die I put my head against the wall and I do my death dance. I move, rocking from side to side until I start to dream, stupidly, of my mother and the hillside and my aunties and my little friends . . .

'I always dream the same dream. Isn't it silly. It is not really a very happy dream because in the end I know what happens, I know the dream so well. It is like spending a day on the hillside in the forest and I no longer care what is happening all around me.'

Sunday Mirror 29 September 1974 (George Martin)
BIG CAT KILLINGS UPSET ZOO MEN
The destruction of five big cats has upset keepers at London's Regents Park Zoo.

Three pumas, a lion and a leopard have been killed at the zoo where the 100-year-old lion house is being modernized.

A lioness, Augusta – known to visitors as Gussie – is due to be put down soon.

After keepers revealed their distress to the Sunday Mirror, Mr Colin Rawlins, the Zoo Director, said yesterday: 'we don't just knock 'em off, as it were, without very careful thought.'

'We have been locked inside all day. There are frantic noises outside. The prisoners are making a noise saying that Toto and Lakshmi were having a row as usual, and either Toto fell or Lakshmi pushed her into the moat. Somehow Toto is still alive. Lakshmi, now back inside and chained, is silent and brooding, but I sense pleasure in her silence, whether she was the cause of it or not.

'I am hearing the most incredible story too – how Toto tried to escape running along the bottom of the moat with a keeper – the one I like – desperately hanging on to her head – her ear. She didn't get very far, only to the young prison visitors playground.'

The Observer 16 October 1983
In the wild Pole Pole would live in a matriarchal all female group. In captivity her only choices are either other elephants or a close bond with one or two keepers. She has neither. Doctor B. Bertram, Curator of mammals at the zoo . . . 'you cannot assess misery in an elephant', he says . . . he concedes, however, that changes of keeper may have unsettled her.

'Time has no meaning in prison, only events punctuate the endless, hopeless, boring days. Each day a similar spread of prison visitors, all standing looking with their lost expressions. Are some of them reaching out, looking for some way to communicate with all the rest of the creatures they visit . . . do they know why they visit us . . . . Some of them look a bit like some prisoners, with their raw, moon-shaped, naked pink faces and awkward jerky movements. They seem to have been born with hardly any hairy covering for their skin, like us – Toto, Anna and me. They cover various parts with grey and brown to make themselves the same colour as us. Some of them cover themselves with the same hair and skin the prisoners

When animals die I put my head against the post and I do my death dance.
(Ian Dobbie)

The prison visitors look at me all the time.   (Ian Dobbie)

have. Perhaps they get them when the prisoners die. It seems strange they would want to look like prisoners! Could it really be that prison visitors love us so much that they keep us in prisons and wear our skins.

'I think many of them have more sorrow for us than love, but perhaps to them there is not much difference.

'The children of prison visitors shout at us a lot and try to make the sounds some prisoners make when they are angry. They seem always to be very hungry. They eat from little packets and drink all day long. Every day is the same.'

The Daily Express 21 October 1983 (George Gale)
HOW CAN WE TREAT ANIMALS LIKE THIS? – If a little bird in a cage puts all Heaven in a rage, what does an elephant in a zoo do to the folks up there?

'Anna is five. She has been here since she was only a few months old. She was adorable as a baby, soft, cuddly, bouncing – not walking – bouncing like an india-rubber ball . . . and so funny sucking her trunk, then standing on it and falling over.

'She loved to tease me . . . but she has changed. She does not laugh any more . . . and neither do I. Oh, she is still nice and quiet and good tempered – she is the only one that is. Toto hates Lakshmi and me. And Lakshmi, well, perhaps it is best just to say that we do not get on at all. No one trusts Lakshmi ever since she nudged Toto into the moat. I do not think it is anyone's fault, it is just this awful prison. All these monstrous, bleak grey shapes, huge fat branchless cement trunks pointing to the sky. No trees. No leafy shade to stand under.'

The Daily Mail 5 October 1982
Sir Hugh Casson (who designed the Regents Park Zoo elephant house) said

that the concrete complex was designed to be as robust as possible. He added: 'Inevitably, any elephant house appears fortified. Elephants are individuals and behave in certain ways which make them not the easiest creatures to deal with – they can even pick locks with their trunks. Everything must be out of their reach' . . . He said: 'It is terribly sad if Pole Pole is pining away.'

'My friendly warder has gone. Warders come and go. I don't know them.

'Toto is dead, yes dead. Well . . . do not look at me. The prison visitors look at me all the time . . . I am not sad . . . not anything. Why should I be. As usual, no one knows how she died. She was in the next cell crying to herself. We felt she was dying some hours before. You can always tell . . . there is such a strange smell when you start to die. Death is terrible. I go frantic. I do not care about Toto . . . I must bang down the iron door. I must get away from that smell! That smell! That sickly stench!

'I found my forehead was bleeding and the warm blood was running into my eyes. I was glad, I thought I was crying . . .'

Letter to Mrs Daphne Sheldrick from Jan Adams, a keeper's fiancée
Then when Toto died (again because of bad design of the house – no way of removing the body), they did the post-mortem in the next den to Pole. You cannot imagine the affect this had on her. She walked round in circles day and night for six weeks till she dropped. It was months before she settled down.

Letter to Mrs J Fudakowska from G. C. G. Rawlins, Director of Zoos, Regents Park, London 13 May 1983
Whatever people may think about 'Pole Pole' and elephants, the great majority of animals in our two Zoos of London and Whipsnade, and indeed in all good zoos round the world, are almost certainly healthier, more secure, more

contented and in general far better off than their brothers and sisters in the
rapidly declining wild.

Letter to Mrs Harris from G. C. G. Rawlins, Director of Zoos 9 February 1983
Pole Pole lived happily and contentedly in the zoo for nearly fourteen years
with her companions. When her close companion died in 1980, we
immediately set about trying to find another place for her to go to.

'The smell of Toto's dead body is everywhere! How can I forget even for
one moment that she is dead. I have to breathe, I have to draw in the stench
of a decaying corpse, the sensation of death.

'They must know what happens to us when one of us dies. They have kept
prisoners like us here for years and years . . . Watching . . . Watching so
many prisoners. They must know. Yes, they know, but they do not feel for
their prisoners. Would they torture us like this if they did? They must see we
go crazy, rush around trying to escape – to escape that terrible sickly smell,
like rotten mangoes, that hot, sour-sweet breath that corpses exhale to
summon flies and maggots to the feast.

'And the prison visitors watching, see us rushing up and down and laugh
at our madness. They don't understand . . . they find it funny, they laugh as
we batter our heads against the iron doors, laugh as we wander round and
round in circles seeking escape, seeking dreams, oblivion.

'I look at *them*.

'I see prison visitors my own age – thirteen, fourteen with their mothers,
laughing, eating. *Don't they mind the hot clammy smell of death?* My mother will
die in some forest . . . why pretend. My mother died in some forest and the
fresh scented breeze washed her body. And all my aunties and friends and
children gathered around to touch her with their trunks, to caress her, to
thank her for her kindness to them, to say goodbye.

'Death is an end to life – frightening but beautiful, I am told, in a forest. And
when they have finished remembering their friends and relations in life, they
carry their huge, long ivory-white teeth to a certain place in the forest to
remember them in death.

'Here in prison you are chopped up to be carted away and forgotten.
Some prisoners, when they die, are chopped up and fed to some other
prisoners. I do not think prison visitors know this, but we do. We even know
which prisoners are in the meat cart. It is lucky we are vegetarians.

'Lakshmi pushed Toto in the trench four years ago – four years ago – and
now suddenly they say she has died of injuries. They know the truth . . . I . . .
wonder . . . Toto was not very old . . . 28 they say. Maybe it is the white
house way to explain so many premature deaths to prison visitors.'

Letter to Mrs Eveleigh from J. Crammond, Press Officer of Zoological Society, London
5 December 1983
You ask us about the death of Toto. She died very suddenly in April 1980,
following a sudden infection.

Letter from Mrs Hennessy (keeper's wife) 3 October 1982
My husband Matthew worked with all three elephants you have mentioned since 1965 and was so upset over the death of Toto (who was his favourite). Matt offered to spend the night with Toto before her death and he was refused by his overseer to stay with her, when she needed someone most of all. It was obvious when her best friend died beside her, in the next den, that Pole went beserk you could say almost mad with sorrow.

'They have not taken Toto's body away. There is the most terrible stench in my cell. They did not take her away. They decided to cut her up into pieces in the next cell to me.'

Iain and Oria Douglas-Hamilton's book *Among the Elephants*
For human beings and for elephants death remains significant in the behaviour of the survivors. In life individuals of both species are tied by strong family bonds and frantic attempts may be made to save a sick or dying relative.

Many great zoologists, including Charles Darwin, have thought that animals possess strong emotions and I have little doubt that when one of their number dies and the bonds of a lifetime are severed, elephants have a similar feeling to the one we call grief. Unfortunately science as yet has no means of measuring or describing emotions even for human beings, let alone for animals.

It is perhaps not surprising that attempts to assist a dying elephant may continue long after it is dead.

'I cannot get the heavy smell of decaying flesh out of my nose. It has seeped through my body into my lungs, so that even my breath smells of poor Toto's rotting body. I can no longer escape into my dream world. I cannot stand this any longer. I rock backwards and forwards near to my droppings, wafting their leafy odour to escape for a moment or two the smell of Toto's chopped up body, but I cannot get away. I charge and batter and hope I will not think or feel.

'I am bleeding again and my face is all bruised and I am standing quite calmly and I do not mind any more. I am so calm . . . I found my dream world again . . . the hillside is so beautiful today in the sun, the forest is alive with birds and creatures that are free.'

Zoological Society of London Annual Report 1980
Other events in the Elephant and Rhino pavilion were the death of the female African Elephant, Toto, from a pulmonary haemorrhage.

'Anna and Lakshmi are making terrible sounds of distress. My grief turns to rage. . . I have to keep running round and round, up and down to stop the pain. I talked to Anna this morning. I heard her calling. I long to see her but we are kept apart. I am alone. Standing. Like when they came and took me away from my family . . . Perhaps they are all dead too. Some prisoners say that their families were all killed, every one of them, and that they can remember seeing their mother and sisters all lying dead . . . bleeding.

Iain and Oria Douglas-Hamilton's book *Among the Elephants*
His [Ian Parker's] method of killing came of long experience of elephant reactions to gunfire. The tame herds of the Park were an easy prey. Cautiously approaching a group, he and his hunters would let the elephants become aware of something unusual by deliberately breaking twigs, making metallic clicks, or coughing gently; hearing this the elephants, sensing an alien, unidentified presence, would invariably move in towards one another forming a defensive circle with mother facing outwards and the young and the babies tucked between their legs or stowed safely behind a mass of body. The hunters would then close in until they were spread in a semi-circle around the tightly bunched elephants and open fire with semi-automatic rifles of the type used by NATO. The largest cows would be shot first, whereupon the younger members of the group would mill about in hopeless confusion, bereft of leadership but unwilling to abandon their dead leaders. The hunters would swiftly finish off the rest. A group of ten animals usually took no more than 30 seconds to kill. No survivors were ever left and consequently the bad news never spread from one group to the next. The only ones sometimes to be spared were calves between the ages of three and seven; old enough to live without milk from their mothers but young enough to be caught and sold to zoos . . . Little of the carcass was wasted. Meat was sold for local consumption around the Park, the feet were made into umbrella stands, and the entire skin and the ears tanned to make an unusually hard-wearing leather. The ivory was the most valuable commodity of all, and found a ready market.
Ian Parker paid the Park five pounds an elephant.

'But my family, I remember them calling, I could not move I was so stupid and frightened. I do not remember my family dying, I do not remember seeing them lying dead and bleeding, but it was so long ago.'

Iain and Oria Douglas-Hamilton's book *Among the Elephants*
The older calves that I studied showed that for at least the first ten years of their life elephants continue to be nurtured by the love and protection of their family. Even when the next sibling is born, the older calf still receives plenty of affection from his mother which goes on until adolescence and in some cases long beyond.

'We have never been so happy Anna and I. We are together again, we do not get on but it is wonderful just being together. I even love all the shoving and jostling . . . of course, Lakshmi is still kept separate. She grumbles and swings her trunk violently to attract attention but we take no notice. Anna chases imaginary warders, not to hurt them — well not really — just to play with them.'

Iain and Oria Douglas-Hamilton's book *Among the Elephants*
Play-fighting must be of functional significance to an elephant; probably teaches an animal its exact strength relative to the others that inhabit the same

area. In this way, through friendly contests in which animals do not get hurt, a hierarchy originates in which each individual knows its place.

'She gets on best of all of us with the warders, she is full of high spirits. I suppose after all these months of disinfectant we hardly notice the smell of Toto's body but the stain is there however hard they clean.

'Of course, you cannot really run properly in prison. The outside area is hardly big enough. Perhaps it is just as well, it is so easy to get pushed down into the trench.

'The summer was warm and long and there were lots of flies, but now they have gone. There has been no sun for days and days. The morning frost has melted but it is very cold. I get quite numb. It is too cold for prison visitors, just a few rubbing their hands, breath clouding their faces . . . and then occasionally I glimpse a figure or two I recognize moving among the bare trees. One of the scientists from the white house . . . wandering round, seeing who has died . . . who is going to.

'The season is over and it is the killing time again. Some must go to make room for those about to be born, some must go because they are old or ill, there just is not room for everyone. Every time I look at Anna I feel hollow and feeble as if I have forgotten how to move. It is because they are looking at her.'

The Zoological Society of London 1979–1981 Scientific Report – Pathology – 1980
The total number of carcasses examined at Regent's Park not excluding those of domesticated species numbered 607. This was a comparable figure with recent years.

'I am learning to trust one of the warders. I know he wants to become my friend but I hit him once when I panicked. He never really showed resentment. People say warders would not be doing the job unless they liked us. Sometimes that is right but I have had one or two beatings. Perhaps it is to appear strong because they are afraid of us and our strength. I try to forget, but for us it is not easy.

'Yes, Lakshmi is going away. It was those men from the white house who came. No one knows where she is going but the prisoners can always tell. They can always tell when someone is going because a crate, another little prison, is brought into the area and the warders start to make a great fuss. Sometimes we can hear prisoners crying inside themselves, in their breathing, even when they are in another cell.'

Letter to Mrs Daphne Sheldrick from Jan Adams 17 July 1982
Shortly after Toto's death, Lakshmi was sent to Rotterdam. The idea now was to get rid of the big untrained elephants and replace them with babies who could be trained.

'The prison visitors seem to know, too, that Lakshmi is going away, they have all started looking at her. It is strange how much fuss is made of you when you are leaving a prison, or dead. Some prison visitors cry when prisoners die so they must love them a bit. . . but why do they keep us prisoner?

Time Out 13 May 1983 (Andrew Tyler)

ELEPHANTS GRAVEYARD

Meanwhile, relations between the elephants were blowing hot and cold. On balance Bertram insists 'they got along'. But during her last year in London, Lakshmi had to be kept separate from the others, spending much of the day as well as the night confined to her pen. And Toto also had to be chained inside to prevent an injury to Pole. These forbidden liaisons within an already cramped enclosure should not be allowed, says Bertram, to discolour our reading of a basically happy picture.'

In 1980 such tensions as did exist were eased with the despatch of Lakshmi to a mating herd in Rotterdam Zoo. Soon after, she was found dead in a moat there. Rotterdam say she had a massive heart attack and fell in – not the other way round, as some have suggested.

Zoological Society of London Annual Report 1980

The adult female Indian elephant, Lakshmi, was sent to Rotterdam Zoo in August to join a group in which she may be able to breed. Her departure eases the management of the elephant and rhino pavilion since she had to be kept apart from the other elephants. Moving proved a major operation. She had to be sedated before she could be moved into the massive crate which then had to be lifted from the enclosure by a very tall crane. The crate was carried to Rotterdam on a low-loader vehicle.

The Zoological Society of London 1979–1981 Scientific Report – Sedation and Anaesthesia

Some of the most interesting findings occurred following the use of the combination of Ketamine and Xylazine, on many occasions in the same animals. The extensive work which was carried out with the Department of Reproduction on the breeding biology of large cats, in particular the Puma and Cheetah, necessitated the sedation of a number of these animals on many hundreds of occasions. . ..

The most interesting individual case of the period was the successful movement under sedation of an adult female Indian elephant from Regent's Park to Rotterdam Zoo in Holland. This animal had a reputation of being difficult to handle. An initial dose of 0.15mg/kg of Xylazine base on an estimated weight of 3,000kg was given to facilitate walking her from her pen into a transport crate, a movement which otherwise would have been impossible with this animal. She was given additional doses of one third of the original level at 2-h intervals throughout the journey to keep her sedated but still standing. Complete recovery occurred shortly after entering her new accommodation at Rotterdam.

The Daily Mail 21 October 1982. *Letter from C. G. C. Rawlins, Director of Zoos*
Lakshmi had a heart attack and then fell into the moat.

'In prison no one does anything. We do not even have the pleasure of finding our own food or water, everything is provided except purpose and hope. . . there is no escape. If you leave one prison it is to go to another. The only real way out is death. Lakshmi was found, they say, in her new prison in Holland, hanging in the moat by a chain attached to one leg. The prisoners say she should have been attached by two chains so she could not fall in the trench but I believe it will be said, as usual, that she died of a heart attack. Poor Lakshmi, she was not very old, just 28. The same age as Toto when she died. 28; 28 – some of my aunties on the hillside were 40 and 50 years old! I will be 15 myself soon.'

The Daily Mail 21 October 1982 *'Elephant Tales'. Letter from C. G. C. Rawlins, Director of Zoos*
Anna was sent to Rotterdam because it is a first-class zoo with a breeding group of Asian elephants and they wanted a female of sub-adult age.

'Why has Anna to go? I have stopped crying. I can bear the loneliness. I tell myself I don't exist and I don't. I don't hear anything any more. They want me to be alone.
'I don't see prison visitors. They are there but I do not see them. If they start to become real I bang my head on the metal door until the sounds and the visitors disappear. I like the smell of my own blood, it tells me that I am alive. The big bosses come and stand in front of me shaking their heads.'

Letter to the Director of London Zoo from A. D. Page, Southsea 19 October 1983
The warning signal sounded two years ago when Virginia McKenna tried so hard to get her released. Your zoo chose to ignore this.

Letter to A. D. Page from London Zoological Society, signed by Joan Crammond for Director of Zoos 24 October 1983
Nowadays, a major zoo like London seeks to advance the welfare of animals through careful Conservation, Research and Education of the public.

'Another year. Yes . . . another year. It is more than a year since Lakshmi died and Anna went. I do not think she is dead, well no one has said so yet. I have got a different warder. He is not my friend and I am not his. I've banged my head so much that my teeth are broken, one of my teeth has come out. I am very ugly. I hope I am. They do not keep you if you are too ugly or ill. The other prisoners say I will soon get the "Big S". I cannot imagine it. I hope it is not very painful. It must feel very strange.'

Letter to Mrs Daphne Sheldrick from Jan Adams, Keeper's fiancée 17 July 1982
Now the arrival of the first baby elephant is imminent. And no other Zoo wants Pole . . . Keepers have come to us and said it is almost certain she will be put down . . .'

I tell myself I don't exist, and I don't. (Ian Dobbie)

Letter to Mrs Daphne Sheldrick from Zoological Society of London 30 July 1982
signed by Doctor B. C. R. Bertram, Curator of Mammals
Whatever you may have heard, there are no plans to put Pole Pole down. I am
not trying to pretend that we would never have to do so, but I can assure you
that we would certainly not contemplate it unless we are [sic] convinced that it
was the best thing for her from the various different options available. We are
most certainly not at that stage at present.

The Sunday Times 3 October 1982 (Brian Jackman)
With her single cracked tusk and deeply wrinkled complexion, she is a slightly
shabby, rather cantankerous and very lonely elephant. . ... When *The Sunday
Times* tried to photograph Bill Travers and Virginia McKenna with Pole Pole
last week, a keeper suddenly appeared and the animal was whisked away
behind closed doors. 'There's only one issue at stake here and that is Pole's
welfare,' said the Zoo's current Senior Veterinary Officer, David Jones.

'Today in my dreams I saw two people who looked like the people who
became my friends when I was a film star, when Eleanor was with me and
life was beautiful. Then I heard their voices. I stopped my pacing up and
down and forced myself to listen. I heard them calling my name. It was
them. They were standing among the prison visitors. I could hardly believe
it. I rushed over to the barrier. I stretched out to touch their outstretched
hands. They were real. I let go of their fingers. It is them. But they are just
like the rest of the prison visitors. They just stand there and look at me. Oh,
I remember my mother running into the forest, I remember. They are still
there. I remember just after I arrived at the prison he brought me a bag of
oranges. He came inside the prison and gave me the oranges and we spoke.
He did not tell me that he would not come back until now, all these years
later.

'I still cannot bear to think about Anna. Why did she have to go. Wasn't it
enough that they took Lakshmi? When Anna knew she was going, deep in
her lovely body she rumbled like thunder in enormous sadness. Sounds that
the warders and prison visitors could hear, and they all watched her. But she
talked to me in sounds only we and the other prisoners know. Anna was not
so sad for herself. She was thinking of us, of me, trying to comfort me. "I am
not going to die like Lakshmi," she said with great seriousness. "So you do
not have to worry," and after a few moments added "and if I do die," and
here tears filled her beautiful eyes, "I will wait for you somewhere Pole.
There has to be somewhere where we can meet again, so cheer up." And
then we both started to cry. "You will not be lonely, Pole," she said, "I am
sure it will not be long. They are always having prisoners like us for the
prison visitors to look at. Some prisoners are already saying that another
baby is to be brought to our cell to replace me."

"Goodbye, Pole . . . I will miss you."

'I was not allowed to see her the day she left.'

I rushed over to the barrier. I stretched out to touch their outstretched hands. (Daily Mail)

Anna, 11 years old, the day before she left for Rotterdam. (Jan Adams)

Letter to Mrs Daphne Sheldrick from Jan Adams 17 July 1982
My fiancé has recently retired as Head Keeper of the elephant house. He is very fond of Pole who is at present the only elephant in the zoo.

Before 1980 there were four, and to cut a long story short, because of the wide difference in their ages, the bad design of the house, and zoo policy, none of them was trained (with the exception of Lakshmi, who had had some training as a baby, but this was not followed up as she was considered dangerous.)

Letter to Mrs Eveleigh from J. Crammond, Press Officer for Regents Park Zoo 22 November 1983
As you know, in future, we plan to train our elephants much more closely, as we are now doing with our young Asian elephant, Dilberta. She goes out into the grounds every day with her keepers and we are confident that this gives her a much more interesting life and also enables her keepers to establish a closer relationship with her.

The Daily Mail 19 October 1983 Virginia McKenna
WHERE I LAY THE BLAME

We've always claimed that Pole Pole should have been sent to Whipsnade at once, to be with her own kind, or back to Africa. Unfortunately, London Zoo's attitude was that we were talking poppycock, were sentimental cranks. . . that we were doing this for personal publicity. . .. We found a South African game reserve where she could have lived happily. The Zoo said Pole Pole would never survive in the wild. But she could have gone to a reserve.

Then they said she would have been killed by poachers, but no poacher would bother with an animal with just one pitiful broken stump of tusk.'

The Times 19 October 1983

He [Bill Travers] and Miss McKenna had been campaigning to have Pole Pole returned to her natural habitat in Africa. But Mr Jones said the zoo had made enquiries and concluded that no suitable place in Africa could be found for her.

Progress Report on the re-introduction of two captive South African elephants into the Pilanesberg Game Reserve, Bophuthatswana, by Randall Moore. Submitted to: Dr Jeremy Anderson Director of the Reserve on 15 May 1983.

Summary. This report was prepared for those persons interested in the process and progress of the first re-introduction of *Loxodanta africana*, from 16 years of captivity, to being fully rehabilitated into the wilds of the Pilanesberg Game Reserve.

After nine months in residence inside the reserve, the elephants have settled-in extremely well. It took a mere two months to wean these gentle giants from a completely artificial diet to one of 100% self selection of natural browse and grazing. After four months the elephants had eaten a total of 35 different plants, and approximately 20 daily, and their number continues to grow.

'Since Anna went, all the prisoners have been talking about me. How long will I be here, they chant. I try not to think about it and run up and down and up and down until the pain goes away, but as I keep running up and down I start to sleep, to dream as I run. At least that is what it feels like. They cannot hurt me when I am dreaming.

'The leaves have all turned yellow and are starting to fall. It is quite cold again. The leaves were falling off the trees a long time ago when Anna left, when Lakshmi died, a long time ago. A long time ago when Toto died. I feel I have been here all my life. I have, I suppose. If I think about it I can remember how to tie a knot in my trunk. This is the most boring place. Nothing changes, just walking up and down and running up and down and battering the doors.'

Iain and Oria Douglas-Hamilton's book *Among the Elephants*
Elephants are intelligent animals which resemble us in some forms of their behaviour.

'There is a smaller prison being moved into the area outside. It looks different from Lakshmi's.'

Time Out October 1983 (Andrew Tyler)

WILL POLE POLE PACK HER TRUNK?

At London Zoo itself, the problem of the actual transit container is being tackled by a commercial company who have constructed a metal crate just wide enough and tall enough to contain the upright Pole without giving her excess room in which to flail.

For more than a week the crate has been stationed on the inside of the pavilion between two sections of sleeping pens – but minus the front and back panels. So positioned it serves as a walk way and Pole is being encouraged to get its feel by crossing through it from one pen section to the other. When the time comes for the move, the keepers will simply draw her in and slide down the front and back panels.

For as long as the crate is in place, however, Pole will not merely be solitary but unable to get outside into the fresh air. The crate blocks off her exit.

'It must be true – no one else would need a travelling prison that big or that strong . . . where they have put it means I have got to walk through the cage to get outside . . how many days will I not want to go outside? How long can I hold out . . . No point . . .

'Where are they taking me . . . I don't suppose they would order a crate if they wanted to kill me. They would just get out the "Big S" . . . yes, *that is right*. . . or I could have a heart attack, I suppose. No, I am definitely going somewhere . . . another prison . . . You would think they would let me go home after all these years. I cannot even remember what I have done to be imprisoned.

'I am not brave really. It is easy to say you are brave . . . don't care, but actually my knees are very wobbly . . . I find I am sucking the tip of my trunk a lot these days. I just feel if I make a mistake now . . . they will kill me. The big bosses in the white house look at me so blankly. I suppose I am just one more prisoner to them, and they have thousands of prisoners here.

'They have been here all day, and I have been locked up in my cell all day. When I came out I had to go through the small prison to get to the exercise yard. At first I thought they were going to lock me up if I tried to pass through it, but they didn't. I was glad to get out, so I wandered through again . . . no doubt they will close the doors when they want to. Why should I forget all the other times I have gone – or been forced – into a little prison before I came here . . . they think I do not remember.

'I feel very sick and dizzy. Those people from the white house give me injections practically every day now and each time I feel ill. Some part of the syringe or something broke off and got stuck in my ear where they inject me.

It aches and throbs. The other prisoners say I am being sent away. Well, I know that, and I do not mind very much but there is such a strange awful familiar smell . . .'

Time Out October 1983 (Andrew Tyler)

WILL POLE PACK HER TRUNK?

One keeper, who declines to be identified, claims that one of these dummy runs went badly wrong when a metal dart fired into a spot behind her left ear broke off and caused a massive swelling. A zoo spokesman confirms that there was a 'boil from an unknown cause' behind her ear, but this has now been drained.

It seems probable that the move to Whipsnade will eventually take place, although by now Pole is increasingly suspicious of her weird human captors and there is no telling how she might respond in transit or upon arrival. She is even reported to have gone down front knees instead of back legs first during one darting rehearsal – a most unusual occurrence and interpreted by two people who have known her well as a last ditch act of defiance by a creature who fears for her life.

'Why do they keep injecting me . . . I can hardly stand up . . . my day dreams are not dreams any more, they are terrifying nightmares. I keep falling down big black holes . . . always falling. The other prisoners were right of course, I am going home after all. After all these years away . . . I am going home.

'I can see the hillside now . . . it is all red in huge black clouds. My mother is there . . . yes, she is there . . . but she is fading . . . disappearing into the red side of the hill . . . there are no trees on the hill, it is very sad . . .

'Standing in my little prison – it is so small – just a few inches above my head and just a few inches wider than I am . . . Oh well, what can I do.

'It is tiny this cage. . . no room to breathe.

'They are shutting the door of my iron cage but I am so dizzy I can hardly stand and my legs feel like jelly. . . I ache all over.

'Oh yes, there is that smell again. I can smell something . . . a strange . . .I must try to stand up or I will never get home . . . home?

'Yes . . . yes . . . . . yes . . . . There is such a deathly silence. I am going home. . . WHY DON'T THE OTHER PRISONERS SPEAK! SPEAK! YOU MUST HEAR! I AM GOING HOME!

You do not believe it do you. Oh, well . . . . Oh dear, I have fallen down – how clumsy.'

The Guardian 12 October 1983 (Penny Chorlton)

Pole Pole, a seventeen-year-old African elephant, sat tight yesterday in a specially designed steel cage (see pictures above) forcing officials at London Zoo to cancel her proposed transfer to the broader pastures of Whipsnade Zoo, Bedfordshire.

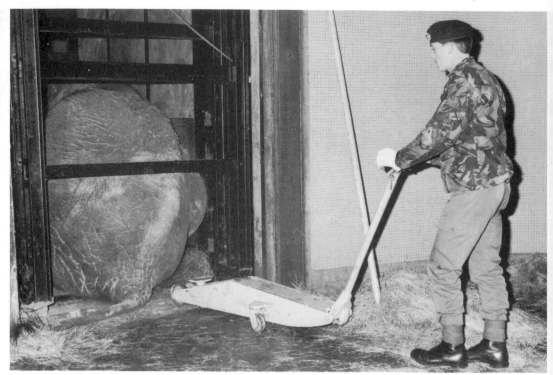

They have got some metal contraption.   (The Press Association)

They believed that it would be too dangerous for her to make the trip lying down, and even members of the Royal Engineers were unable to persuade the elephant – whose name means Slowly Slowly in Swahili – to get on to her feet.

London Zoo officials say that the half acre paddock at Whipsnade – which she will share with three other elephants – will be the best home for Pole Pole. 'That is as much space as any captive animals have in the world,' says Doctor Brian Bertram, chief Curator of Mammals.

The Zoological Society of London 1979–1981 Scientific Report – Pathology 1979
During the period 1 January to 31 December 1979 inclusive, 838 post-mortem examinations were carried out at Whipsnade Park (Table XV). These included three wild mammals and two wild birds found in the Park and twelve external cases.

Table XV
Post-mortem examinations at Whipsnade 1979

	Acclimatized	Unacclimatized	Neonate/ Stillborn	Total
Mammalia	637(9)	0	41	678

Figures in brackets denote euthanasia primarily for management purposes.

. . . too ill. I cannot move. (The Press Association)

'They keep looking at me – the big bosses – scientists – and then looking at their watches. They look very anxious as if something has gone wrong.

'. . . What are they waiting for?

'I do not seem to be able to move. I am very strong really . . .

'They have got some metal contraption, a lifting device to try to get me up . . . but I am sorry, I am sorry I am too ill. I cannot move.

It is all those injections . . . that throbbing in my ear.

'I cannot move . . . Where am I . . . it is my cell . . . they must have done it while I was asleep . . . but I cannot get up . . . I try . . . I know I must. . . . HELP ME!

'The big bosses – the scientists – are all standing around me . . . looking at me. Shaking their heads . . . shaking their heads . . .

'It is dark . . . black clouds on the red hillside . . . it must be the middle of the night. I have been asleep.

'I am not really bothered about them . . . big bosses . . . It is that awful smell . . . that sickly sweet stench . . .

'One of them is coming towards me. He has a syringe in his hand . . . a big syringe . . . Oh, I know that smell so well.

'Oh yes . . . yes . . . I understand, this is it . . . "The Big S" . . .

'They are fumbling . . . their bodies smell moist . . . I suppose . . . suppose . . . they are nervous too.

'Oh God, yes . . . yes, AAAH . . .

'I can feel the prick. It is hot and burning . . . Oh God, Oh God . . . but it is all right really, it is . . .

' It is all right, it is all right, it is all right . . .

At last. It . . . is . . . all . . . right . . . Anna . . . I . . . am . . . going . . . home . . .'

Time Out 28 October to 2 November 1983, letter from member of the public.

RIP Pole Pole

I was deeply saddened by the news of the death of Pole Pole the African elephant, not because she is dead — it can only be a relief to her — but because London Zoo *started* killing her 15 years ago.

For years, Pole Pole was shut up in a concrete prison, wearing her poor skin against its walls, for the simple reason that she had committed the crime of being created a wild animal. They denied her wildness, they punished her for her wildness and they have murdered her for her wildness. She never had the grass beneath her feet, the space around her which her great size was bestowed upon her to use, the companions of her own breed to share the world with her. She never had anything because she was just a money-taking exhibit. I am utterly disgusted by this horrible, horrible story, and I am utterly disgusted by man's inhumanity everywhere towards the animals he is supposed to be caring for. The human race makes me sick. What kind of a world is my child going to grow up in? By the time he is an adult, there will be nothing left that's good and natural and, above all, wild. Nothing at all.

Anne Layram, London N3.

...ests after the death of zoo ...hant that got stuck in crate

...OLE POLE HAS TO BE PUT DOWN

by Colin Adamson and Julie Fairhead

LONDON Zoo's giant elephant Pole Pole, who became trapped in a crate last week, has had to be put down.

The Zoo said the 17-year-old African elephant "lost the will to live" after damaging a foot during an attempt to move her to Whipsnade.

Pole Pole, pronounced Poly Poly, was given a lethal injection last night when she failed to regain her feet after being anaesthetised for an exploratory operation.

Zoo officials had tried for hours to raise the four-ton elephant.

Animal freedom campaigners immediately protested at the way Pole Pole — which means Slowly Slowly in Swahili — was treated.

Actress Virgi... who starred in a wild-life film in Keny... featuring Pole Pole, broke down in... news.

Campai...

Miss Mc...
...ers had...

VIRGINIA McKENNA: in tears.

...McKenna and Bill Travers
Virginia McKenna was "completely shattered" on hearing the news of her death. "I pray," she said, "they never have another elephant at London Zoo."
...ondon Zoo — who have recently

Afte... for c...

LONDON Zoo, ...
over its decision la...
put down its Africa...
Pole Pole, is comi...
increasing pressur...
Whitehall to refor...
shackle managemen...
if it is to continue t...
Treasury support.

Its annual deficit i...
running at just under £2...
a year. This is being me...
Government on a ten...
year-by-year basis. Earl...
year, the Zoo...
asking...

FRO...
ELEPHANT'S
...ONCL...

...illed off their last
...ole Pole, on Tues-
...ione of elephants,
...ay, was schedu-
...shed after the
...r foot following

...e away for some
...n for an intended
...dragged on. For
...been confined to
...without fresh air
...was tried and
...ors of Tuesday
...but down on the
...crate positioned
...ters.

...municated as an
...who
...were afoot for
...at she had been
...with etorphine.
...ae some ten.
...ns gave way.
...Our the fol-
"quite well
...and 'not at all
...announcing
...she had been

...and unhappy
...ephants live
...Our last
...As Elephant
...led Slowly", a film by Virginia

The la...
...soaked u...
...have int...
...petent to...
...creature...

Zoo's lonely

AFTER THE TRAGIC DEATH OF POLE POLE, THE QUESTION WE MUST ANSWER

Are Britain's zoos really prisons?

By JEREMY GATES

ARE zoos fit places to keep animals?

That's the question thrown up by the tragedy of Pole Pole, the London Zoo elephant who lay down to die.

Even the Government is worried. Their Zoo Licensing Act which comes into operation next year could force many to close.

Zoos will be more rigorously inspected by the authorities. But the fundamental question of how best to keep animals in captivity remains.

Pole Pole was born free in the African bush and died in London. Is her death just one example of how we confine animals, in prisons of misery merely for our entertainment?

Rethink

Yesterday Stefan Ormrod, chief wildlife officer with the RSPCA, had no doubt. "The ...

their captivity and everybody's fairly happy.

"We can't do it with elephants, probably because of their sheer size and strength."

But would people accept that? A London Zoo spokesman said yesterday: "The view of the great British public is that a zoo is not a zoo without the top ten animals, and the elephant is among that top ten.

"We keep elephants for that reason, and we are stuck between two wings of public opinion because of it." They admit "with hindsight" that they might have handled Pole Pole differently and have now changed their ...thods of dealing with

pose it must be education rather than entertainment.

That is London Zoo ...declared purpose. It firm... refuses the suggestion that ...is in the business of us... animals as entertainment.

It forms part of ... Zoological Society of Lo... an educational charit... scientific society set... 1826. With its own I... of Zoology, the zoo i... ably the world's ... research centre and p... the International Zo... which goes around t...

LONDON ...
lonely ele...
Pole has ...
death.

Pole Pole ...
to live afte...
years ago. T...
favourite kee...
and she wa...
the elephant ...

Actress...

ELEPHANT GRAVEYARD

ole Pole: Time
nge at the Zoo

AURENCE MARKS,
EOFFREY LEAN
d ROBIN McKIE
the controversy
rounding London Zoo

An elephant's unhappy life

a hum...
lock...
Kin...
tre...
m...

kept in the concrete and brick
elephant house, which Mr
Jones said was unsuitable for
wild, untrained animals.
"It was built for tame
...hants, and it is fine for

really be kept success
captivity."

He and Miss McKer
been campaigning to ha
Pole returned to her
habitat in Africa. But N
said the zoo had made
and concluded that no
place in Africa could
for her.

Plans were made to
instead to Whips
week the
d in a

must give it something in
n: an interesting environ-
the companionship of
s, and prop...
health care, he
on to stick
ave them.'

de obvio
but m
devilled
entali
on

jection finally put
17-year-old
egent's
on

s a baby by a cull
tial mates
Pole
d

DAILY EXPRESS
Wednesday October 19 1983 • 18p • TV Pages 26 and 27
THE VOICE OF BRITAIN

Zoo is forced to put down the film star
elephant who pined for her dead mate

The short, sad
life of Pole Pole

She lost the will to
live after injury

By JOHN BURNS

.20.
or
is ridicul...

What worries w...
Zoo's ability to adapt its stil...
as a learned society to its need to
compete as a popular
entertainment.

It is governed by a council of 21,
half of them respectable scientists,
the other half notable public
figures like the Duke of Welling-
ton, Mr Justice Waterhouse and
r Philip de Zulueta, a diplomat-
med-financier. There are 2,500

Humber...
Authority.
The professional sta...
by Colin Rawlins, direc
and John Hearn, scien
tor, are in day-to-d
They propose initia
council and put forw
of fellows to serve
committees from

zoo officials last
selves

from importing any more. An indep-
dent inquiry into
undertakes
examine their

death must be
the process

VOICE OF BRITAIN

DAILY MIRROR, Wednesday, October 19, 1983 PAGE 7

ephant
dead

SIMON FERRARI

s never trained
ause it used to be
cy not to tame wild
als.

entually she became
tremely dangerous,"
zoo's chief vet, Dr
d Jones, said yes-
ay.

t it was impossible to
a safe place for her in

Africa and it was decid
to move her to the bett
facilities at Whipsna
Zoo in Bedfordshire.
Pole Pole was load
into a special crate
Monday last week. A
hours later she la
down—and never got
again despite long battles
to raise her.

Pole Pola, aged 17, was
given a lethal injection on
Monday night.

Zoo time is just
a life in prison

YOU EXPRESS YOUR VIEWS

IN VIEW of the public's concern over Pole Pole, the
African elephant who "sat down to die," in London
Zoo, isn't it about time we questioned the need to
keep our zoos open
They are, after all, basically a form of entertainment, and by that token it seems a little uncivilised
that caged animals should be thought of as "fun to look
at" on a par with tele-
vision.
I accept that certain
species of animals are near
extinction and have to be
conserved, but I feel we owe
the animals a little more than
a concrete box in which to
spend their lives.

weren't handli
zoo closely. The
to be trained. C
Pole Pole wil

MUST WE
DO THIS TO
ANIMALS
FOR FUN?

Mrs JANET FITZSIMMONS,
..., West

PHANT

DEATH OF ELEPHANTS IN LONDON ZOO (REGENTS PARK)
1946–1983

Died	Name	Age	Reason or reason given for death
1946	RANEE	10	DIED. Reason not recorded.
1951	RAJAH	12	SHOT – seriously injured two keepers.
1967	DIKSIE	27	DIED – fell in moat.
1969	RUSTY	27	SHOT suspected TB and foot rot.
1980	TOTO	20	DIED Lung haemorrhage and bruising, said to be result of falling in zoo moat four years earlier.
1980	LAKSHMI	28	Transferred to Holland where she was said to have been found DEAD hanging by one chained leg in moat. London Zoo says she had heart attack before falling.
1983	POLE POLE	17	KILLED by lethal injection when she could not get to her feet.

They gave their lives for conservation. So that men women and children might be educated and amused.

Elephants can live to 50 or 60 years old in the wild – in their natural environment.

The Guardian 19 October 1983 *Mr David Jones, Senior Veterinary Officer, London Zoo,*
'Mr Travers has no experience of running an elephant house. In the last 150 years, most of our elephants have died of old age.'

London Zoo Guide
Above all, Zoos are fun.

Zoo News
Our aim is to make Zoos hum with fun. Just enjoy yourself.

Zoo 2000 Jeremy Cherfas (BBC Publications, 1984)
Quite honestly there can be no rational reason for saving wild life in zoos.
The best reason to conserve animals in zoos is simply that it gives us pleasure.

Index

Bold entries refer to illustrations.

Adams, Jan, 183, 187, 189, 194
Adams, Richard, 15, 67
Adamson, George, 25, 90, 129
Adamson, Joy, 25, 59
Adaptation to captivity, 50-2
Agroforestry, 158
Animal
　'adoption', 32
　behaviour, 31, 48-52, 84, 89, 116
　imagery and Christianity, 73-6
　management in zoos, 14, 47-8, 173
　Rights, 17, 38, 86-8
　symbolism cult, 69-70
　welfare, 47
　see also Lobbying
Animals (Scientific Procedure) Bill, 87
Anti-vivisection Groups, 86-8
Attenborough, David, Life on Earth, 99

BBC Wildlife, 13
Behaviour of captive animals, 31, 48-52, 84,
　88-9
　patterns, 116
Belle Vue Zoo, 15, 85
Bertram, Dr Brian, 180, 191, 198
Birds, 86, 89, 117, 120, 120, 126-7
Boredom of zoo animals, 31, 50, 52
Born Free, 25, 129
Boyes, Roland, 15-16, 85
Breeding, captive, 12, 21, 152-3
　cost of, 153
　for reintroduction to wild, 14-15, 45,
　135, 146-7
　for research, 61-2
　selective, 58
Brewer, Stella, 59

Callaghan, James, 110
Campaigning groups, 107
　see also Lobbying
Campbell, Joseph, Masks of God, The, 69
Captive behaviour, 31, 48-52, 84, 88-9

Captive breeding see Breeding, captive
Captivity
　acceptable standards for, 47-8
　animal's reaction to, 50-2
　cruelty of, 34
　and mental illness of animals, 28-9,
　48-52, 88-9, 177
　and repetitive behaviour, 84
　see also Breeding, captive;
　Suffering of captive animals; Zoos
Casson, Sir Hugh, 170
Caufield, Catherine, In the Rainforest, 99,
　150
Cherfas, Jeremy, 58, 61-2, 65, 204
Chester Zoo, 13, 42-3
Chimpanzees, 42-3, 59, 60, 61-2, 114,
　155-16, 119-20
Chipperfield, Richard, 15
Christianity and animal imagery, 73-6
Circus, 15, 82, 83, 85-6, 134-5
Climate and tropical rainforests, 156
Conservation
　defined, 16
　economics of, 92-3, 158
　of environment, 55-7, 65
　of habitat, 34, 36, 45
　need to rationalize, 131-3
　of plants, 121-2
　of species, 55-7, 65
　and zoo purpose, 13
Crammond, Joan, 184-5, 189, 194
Cruelty and captivity, 34, 36-8
　see also Suffering of captive animals

Daily Express, 59, 171, 177, 182
Daily Mail, 168, 183, 189
Deforestation, 16-17, 19-21, 149-50, 151
　see also Tropical rainforests
Development, economic, 92-3
Dignity of animals, 82-4, 134-5
Douglas-Hamilton, Iain and Oria,
　Among the Elephants, 163, 185, 186, 195

Earth, exploitation of, *see* Resources
Earthlife, 36
East African Standard, 162, 167, 168, 175
Economics of conservation, 92-3, 158
Education and Zoos, 12, 13, 45
Egyptian religion, ancient, 69-70
Elephant, **27, 37,** 44, **82,** 88, 130, **132, 162,
    170, 176, 178, 182-3, 194,**
    see also Polc Pole
Emotional feelings of animals, 116, 185
    see also Mental illness in captive animals
Endangered species
    protection of, 16, 86, 89
    reintroduction to wild, 12, 58-60, 89,
        135, 137-43
    see also: Breeding, captive;
        Species
Enquiry systems, 104-6
Entertainment and zoos, 13, 31-2, 34, 82,
    85-6
Environment
    conservation of, 55-7, 65
    zoo, 50-2
    see also Habitat
Erwin, Terry, 149
Eveleigh, Mrs, 184, 194
Evening News, The, 177
Evolution, 99, 116-18
Extinction, 145-6
    see also: Endangered Species;
        Species

Factory farming, 86
Farmers, forest, 158
    and deforestation, 151
Films, wildlife, 11-12, 13, 18, 32, 118,
    125-6
Finance
    better use of, 18, 34, 100, 127
    and breeding, 61
    and conservation, 90, 118, 151, 158-9
    and Third World, 92-3, 127
Friedman, Stanford, 58
Fudakowska, J., 183
Fur trade, **106-7,** 127
    see also: Hunting; Lobbying

Geldof, Bob, 111
Gene-pool, captive, 57-8
Giraffe, **20, 30, 46**
Glover, Mark, 16-17, 97
Goodall, Jane, 62
Governments
    attitude of, 86-7, 111-12

and conservation policies, 93-4
'Greenhouse effect', 101, 156-7
Greenpeace, 17, 95, 104, 110
Guardian, The, 197, 204
Gorillas, **31, 53, 57,** 60, **136**
    Guy the Gorilla, 135, **136**

Habitat
    destruction of, 56-7, 92, 146
    need for, 63
    preservation of, 34, 36, 45
Hardy, Thomas, 73, 78
Harris, Mrs, 184
Hennessy, Mrs, 185
Horsman, Paul, 28
Housing, animal, **43,** 47, 52, **86,** 89, **88,** 89,
    170, 173
Hunting, 19, **81,** 102-3, **103,** 104, **105,
    106-7, 118-19,** 119-20, 127, 130-1,
    132
    'sport', 123-4, **124, 125,** 130, 133-4

Individual, power of, 17, 108-11
    see also Lobbying
International Union for the Conservation of
    Nature   and   Natural   Resources
    (IUCN), 16, 130, 146
International Whaling Commission (IWC),
    102

Jersey Wildlife Preservation Trust, 12
Jersey Zoo, 31, **31**
Jones, Dr David, 168, 191, 204
Jordan, Bill, 13-14, 21, 41
    effect of safari on, 43-5
Jung, C. G., *Memories, Dreams and Reflec-
    tions,* 79-80
Justification for zoos, 12, 13, 19, 31, 45, 56,
    89, 118-19, 135

Keepers, 47, 48
Kenyatta, President, 164, 167

Lawick, Baron Hugo van, 17-18, 115
Lee, F. H., *Folk Tales of All Nations,* 68
Leopard, 130, 133, 137
Lever, Sir Christopher, 11
    Mandarin Duck, The, 23, **22**
Lion Country Safari, 134
Lions, **24, 28,** 47, 59, 129, 130
Lobbying, parliamentary, 16, 86, 104, 107
    tactics of, 94-5, 108
Logging, 150-1, **150, 152**
    changes in methods of, 157-8

London Zoo, 26, 29, 32, 164
Lucknow Zoo, 142

Masks of God, The, (Campbell), 69
McKenna, Virginia, 12-13, 21, 25, 164, 167, 173, 191, 195
Medicine and endangered plants, 121, 155-6
Mental illness in captive animals, 28-9, 48-52, 88-9, 177
  see also Pole Pole
Meyers, Dr Norman, 152, 158
  Primary Source, The, 151
Midgley, Mary, 14-15, 55
Milligan, Spike:
  Amen, 144
  Last Leopard in the Cape, 113
  Whales, 66
Mineral reserves, loss of, 100
  see also Resources, destruction of
Morris, Desmond, 173
Monkeys, **39, 40, 48, 51,** 115
  see also Chimpanzees; Gorillas
Mulvaney, Kieran, 19-21, 145

National Parks, 18, 90, 127-8
  see also Sanctuaries, animal
National Trust, 12
Nature Conservancy Council, 12
Nutrition of zoo animals, 47-8

Observer, The, 168, 173, 188

Phoenix Zoo, 147
Plants, preservation of, 121-2
  see also Tropical rainforests
Polar Bears, 28-9, 43, **43,** 88-9
Pole Pole (elephant), 26, 161-204, **163, 165, 166, 169, 172, 181, 190, 192, 198, 199**
Pollution, **93,** 100-102, **101, 110,** 146
Poverty and deforestation, 151
  see also Finance
Predators, misguided attitudes to, 122-3
Private Eye, 171
Protest groups, 104, 109-110
  see also Lobbying
Public awareness, 59, 95-6, 119
Public opinion, 18, 19, 38, 108-111, 127, 60
Purpose of Zoos *see* Justification for Zoos

Rainbow Warrior, 110
Rainforest *see* Tropical rainforest
Ranching and deforestation, 149-50, 151
Rawlins, Colin, 13, 39, 180, 183-4, 189

Reintroduction of endangered species, 12 58-60, 89, 135, 137-43
Religion and animals, 15, 67-84
Repetitive behaviour *see* Behaviour of Captive animals
Research, 13, 16, 45, **87**
  breeding animals for, 61-2
  and zoo function, 12
Resources, destruction of, 92-3, 99-103
  see also: Deforestation; Habitat
Rhinos, 32, **35, 118-19,** 132-3
  see also Tsavo Rhino Sanctuary
Rotterdam Zoo, 187, 188-9
Royal Society for Nature Conservation, 12
Royal Society for the Prevention of Cruelty to Animals, 106
Royal Society for the Protection of Birds, 12, 26

Safaris, wildlife, 12
San Diego Zoo, 12, 19, 31, 135, 147
Sanctuaries, animal, 16, 34-6
  see also: National Parks; Tiger Haven Range; Tsavo Rhino Sanctuary
Scott, Sir Peter, *The Eye of the Wind,* 18
Sheldrick, Daphne, 165-6, 167-8, 173, 179, 183, 187, 191, 194
Sheldrick, David, 165, 179
Singh, Arjan, 18-19, 129
Soil, destruction and erosion of, 92, 154, 155
Species
  conservation of, 55-7, 65
  extinction of, 145-6, 147
  value of, 63
  see also Endangered species
Stereotypy, 89
Suffering of captive animals, 28-9, 31, 38, 48-52, 88-9, 173
Sunday Mail, 180
Sunday Mirror, 180
Sunday Times, 177, 191
Surrogate motherhood, 62

Tara the tigress, 137-43, **138, 141**
Third World countries and foreign exchange, 92, 127
  see also Finance
Thomas, Keith, *Man and the Natural World,* 81
Tiger Haven Range, 129, 138, 143
Tigers, **10,** 134, 137-43, **138, 141, 142**
Time Out, 163, 164, 165, 167, 170, 196, 197, 201

Times, The, 15, 177
Tinberg, Professor, 49
Tolstoy, Leo, *War and Peace,* 79
Tourism, 18, 127, 132
Trapping animals, 61, 119-21, 127, 128
  see also: Fur trade; Hunting
Travers, Bill, 21, 25, 161, 164, 167, 173, 191
Tropical rainforest, destruction of, 19-21, 99-100, 147-52, **148, 150, 152,** 154-8, **156**
  see also Deforestation; Habitat
Tsavo National Park, 179
Tsavo Rhino Sanctuary, 12, 34, 58, 90

United Nations Development Project, 130
United Nations Environment Programme, 130
United Nations Food and Agriculture Organization, 99, 158

Value of wild life, 91
Veterinary care for zoo animals, 48

Washington Wildlife Park, 89
Whipsnade Zoo, 195, 197, 198

Wildfowl Trust (Slimbridge), 147
Wildlife and Countryside Act, 89
Woburn Abbey, 147
World Conservation Strategy (WCS), 91
World Index of Strategic Minerals, 100
World Wildlife Fund, 36, 130
Worship, primitive, 68

Zoo Check, 12, 13, 26, 28, 29
Zoo Licensing Act, 16, 28, 47
Zoological Society of London, 170, 175, 185, 187, 188, 189, 191, 198
Zoos
  and animal management, 14, 47-8, 173
  and animal suffering, 28-9, 31, 38, 48-52, 88-9, 173
  environment, 50-2
  justification for, 12, 19, 31, 45, 56, 89, 118-19, 135
  keepers, 47, 48
  as living museum, 153-4
  origin of, 45
  see also: Behaviour of captive animals; Breeding, captive; Dignity of animals; Emotional feelings of animals; Pole Pole